Writing Fiction
for
All You're Worth

James Scott Bell

Compendium Press

Also by James Scott Bell

On Writing:

Plot & Structure
Revision & Self-Editing for Publication
The Art of War for Writers
Conflict & Suspense

Fiction:

One More Lie
Watch Your Back
Deceived
Try Dying
Try Darkness
Try Fear
Pay Me in Flesh (as K. Bennett)
The Year of Eating Dangerously (as K. Bennett)
I Ate the Sheriff (as K. Bennett)
City of Angels
Angels Flight
Angel of Mercy
A Greater Glory
A Higher Justice
A Certain Truth
Glimpses of Paradise
No Legal Grounds
The Whole Truth
Presumed Guilty
Sins of the Fathers
Breach of Promise
Deadlock
The Nephilim Seed
Blind Justice
Final Witness
Circumstantial Evidence
The Darwin Conspiracy

Table of Contents

In Defense of How-to-write Books

Every now and again I hear some author putting down how-tos. "You can only learn to write by writing," they'll say. "Don't waste your time studying writing books. Just put a page in front of you and write!"

Which strikes me as making as much sense as saying, "You can only learn to do brain surgery by doing brain surgery. Don't waste your time studying brain surgery. Just cut open heads and go!"

Excuse me if I show a preference for a sawbones who has studied under the tutelage of experienced surgeons.

Another trope is, "No one ever learned to write by reading about writing." Really? Isn't that a bit cheeky, unless you've interviewed every published writer out there?

The writer I know best – me – absolutely learned to write by reading how-tos. I had been fed the bunk that "writers are born, not made" while in college, and I bought it, in part because I took a course from Raymond Carver and couldn't do what he did. (I didn't know at the time that there was more than one way to "do" fiction. I thought everybody had to pass through the same tunnel.)

When I finally decided I had to try to learn to write, even if I never got published, I went after it with a club. I started gathering books on writing, read *Writer's Digest* religiously (especially Lawrence Block's fiction column), took some classes, and wrote every day. Living in L.A. it was required that I try screenwriting first, so I wrote four complete screenplays in one year, giving them to a film school friend, who patiently read them and told me they weren't working. *But he didn't know why.*

Then one day I read a chapter in a book by the great writing teacher Jack Bickham. And I had an epiphany. Literally. Light bulbs and fireworks went off inside my head, and I finally *got it.* Or at least a big part of it.

So I wrote another screenplay, and that was the one that my friend liked. The next one I wrote got optioned, and the one after that got me into one of the top agencies in Hollywood.

After a couple of frustrating years I tried my hand at writing a novel. It sold. Then I got a five book contract, and I was on my way as a working novelist.

In great part because I finally got it from a how-to book.

That's not to say I might not have gotten it some other way (like trial and error over ten years), but at the very least my study program saved me time. And that's the reason I write the occasional how-to book – to save writers time, and give them the nuts and bolts they need to make it in this racket. I want to write the sort of books I was looking for when I was wandering in the darkness.

Apparently it's helped. *Plot & Structure* (Writer's Digest Books), which came out in 2004, was the decade's #1 bestselling book on the craft of fiction writing. As of this writing, it is still #1. Appearing regularly on amazon.com's top ten list in the same category are my *Revision & Self-Editing* and *The Art of War for Writers*.

I keep hearing from people who have sold books based on what they learned from me.

So I repeat: the bromide that you can't learn to write fiction from writing books is the bunk.

How did the writers of the past learn? Many of them had a great editor, like Max Perkins. Some had an older writer who read their stuff and suggested ways to make it better. Some, like the great writer-director Preston Sturges, learned from the how-to books available in his day. (In Sturges's case, it was the books of Brander Matthews.)

So a good how-to book is like an editor or teacher. Is there not some value in that?

Now it is quite true you can't just read how-tos and get better without practice. You have to write every day, and apply what you're learning. But if you write blindly, without correction and education, you're most likely going to be turning wheels like that rodent in the cage. A lot of

3

effort but getting nowhere.

I am a firm believer in how-to books, and write them because I want to give back something to the craft I love.

And that's why I've made this book available. It is a collection of some of my past articles posted on the internet, primarily in the group blog *Kill Zone*. To this content I've added practical application exercises, additional articles and notes.

As a writer, my philosophy is this: if I can find even one thing in a how-to that helps me, that elevates my writing and makes it stronger, it's worth it.

In that spirit I offer this to you. I think you will find more than one thing of value here, and I think it will be worth it to you.

Keep writing.

James Scott Bell

The Never-Ending Writing Improvement Program

In Japan, after World War II, the concept of *kaizen* was introduced into their industrial culture. It resulted in a huge boom in technology and manufacturing that rebuilt Japan and made her prosperous.

It's a simple idea. It means ongoing quality, and systems set up to test quality all the time. And, every day, striving to do something better.

Why should a writer do any less?

You are responsible for designing your own writing improvement program. One that never ends.

To do that, you have to look at both yourself and your fiction. And you have to take the "critical success factors" of each and figure out ways to make them better.

But most writers don't think in a *kaizen* type of manner. We are artists, after all! We want to frolic in the tulip fields of the imagination! We don't want to get weighed down with things like, yikes, strategic planning! We could have gone to engineering school if we wanted to do that kind of thing.

Come on there, Bunkie. It's not that difficult.

Here's the idea. Even if you improve an area only 10%, if you do that with each factor you are improving yourself in an exponential fashion. That's how to get intentional about your career.

The Six Critical Success Factors of Writers

Here are the six areas you need to excel in if you're going to make it as a writer:

1. Craft knowledge

2. Discipline

3. Perseverance

4. Risk

5. Market sense

6. Professionalism

Let's break these down.

Craft knowledge

Mastery of the craft, the tools and techniques of fiction, is of course essential to your success. If you don't know how to put together a scene, or show instead of tell, or construct crisp dialogue, or any of the other nuts and bolts, it's over. You won't write salable fiction.

Keep learning your craft. Do it systematically. At the start of my career, I created a Writing Improvement Notebook (see *The Art of War for Writers* for details of what's in this notebook). Do the same. Make it your own, use it. Spend time in it every week.

Discipline

This means, simply but powerfully, a quota of words. Every week. I split my writing week into six days, and go for 1,000 words a day. But I track it weekly, so if I miss a day I know I can make it up later. I take Sundays off from writing, to recharge my batteries. (Discipline is also about working smarter, not just harder).

Produce the words. There is no substitute for this. Even if your quota has to be small because of your circumstances, pick a number that works, and stretches you just a bit. Then go for it, week in and week out.

Perseverance

Nothing in the world can take the place of persistence. Talent will not; nothing is more common than unsuccessful men with talent. Genius will not; unrewarded genius is almost a proverb. Education will not; the world is full of educated derelicts.

Persistence and determination alone are omnipotent. - Calvin Coolidge

Old "Silent Cal" Coolidge wasn't given to many words, but these are choice. You've got to stay in this deal for the long haul, and determine that from the start. Or *right now.*

You have to know this business is practically all about setbacks and overcoming them: rejections, waiting, criticism, more rejections, more waiting. Just determine you're not going to stop. Ever.

The worst that will happen? You've written a lot of things. What's wrong with that?

Risk

You have to stretch as a writer. Not so far that you tear all your muscles. You don't try to pole vault twenty feet if your personal best is ten.

But to write for all you're worth you need to go a little further. You need to reach further than your grasp. Take risks with your characters, plots, settings, research. Go deeper. Because if you don't, you're just producing what people can get elsewhere. Vanilla.

Market Sense

Headline: publishers and agents want to make money. In fact, they need to make money, or they go out of business.

It's not a bad thing to make money. If you want to write and not get paid, you can skip this section. In fact, you can skip the whole book. It's not for you. The book for you is

Being the Town Eccentric for Dummies.

If you do want to make money as a published writer, you should constantly be asking this question: *who on Earth would pay good money to read what I'm writing?*

The Seven Critical Success Factors of Fiction

1. Plot

2. Structure

3. Characters

4. Scenes

5. Dialogue

6. Voice & Style

7. Meaning (or theme)

The material in this book will help you in each of these areas. But you should assess yourself objectively. Make a list, from your strongest point to your weakest. Then: begin with your weakest area and start working on it. And so on up the list.

That's how you run a never ending writing improvement program. Run it.

The Writing World

Heraclitus (c. 470 B.C.) was a Greek philosopher who observed, "Everything flows, nothing stands still." In other words, change is the only constant in the world. Like a river. "You cannot step into the same river twice," was his favorite bumper sticker. You could see them on the backs of chariots all over Athens.

Similarly, you cannot now step into the same publishing business twice. The writing world is changing so fast that by the time you read this there will be new developments that need analyzing.

Some things remain constant, like the fundamentals of good storytelling. That's what this book is mainly about.

But you have to be up on this swirling river of change if you're going to continue writing for all your worth. Let's break it down.

The Digital Revolution

As soon as books left paper for electricity we entered a cataclysm of change, the like of which hasn't been felt since Gutenberg. Along with what some call a "tsunami" of change come many questions, such as:

* what will a new publishing model look like?

* what's a fair royalty rate for authors giving e-book rights?

* how are prices going to be set in such a way as to give a reasonable return to both authors and publishers?

* what about digital piracy? If people can illegally download music, why can't they do the same with e-books? And if this becomes widespread, how will writers make any money? It's not like musicians, who can play concerts.

* how will e-books affect actual reading habits, and how can authors adjust as a result?

While these questions are being hashed out, there are interesting possibilities for writers:

* writers can go directly to e-publishing outlets, thus cutting out the "middle man."

* e-books can include "enhanced content," such as links, videos and photography, that will give readers a reason to

pay a little more than for a simple e-book.

But there are temptations and dangers included, too:

* writers who aren't ready will rush to self-publishing in digital format, diluting the good stuff and hurting their own careers.

* even established authors may short circuit their work, not getting the editing they need to keep up the quality level.

* quality of design remains an issue. There is nothing so off putting as the cover of most self-published books. If it looks like amateur hour, no one's going to buy.

* marketing is a bigger issue. How to get potential readers to consider your work?

With all that in mind, what can you do *now* to survive in the rushing river of change?

1. You can read. All the time. Find blogs and sites that discuss e-books and read them regularly.

2. Create a business plan with as much care as an entrepreneur starting up a new company. Don't "wing it." Don't rush into e-books. Don't think that just because it's "out there" people are going to find you and buy you. And don't think that if they find you , buy you and think you're not ready for prime time, that they'll ever give you a second chance.

Your business plan should be done in conjunction with

people who know what's going on, like your agent. If you don't have an agent, find people who have some background in business and talk to them.

And you need to think about your "brand."

Branding is a term used by the traditional publishing world to sell authors. Its meaning is quite simple. It refers to what the readers expect and desire from an author as his base grows.

Thus, John Grisham built up a brand as a fast paced, legal thriller writer. Stephen King became a brand name in horror. Nicholas Sparks writes weepies.

So readers looking for the next Grisham or King would be expecting the same kind of ride. And if they got it, they'd talk about the experience, building ever more readers for the authors.

Early in their careers, it was important for Grisham and King to remain "on brand." Maybe Grisham wanted to write a more literary novel. But the publishers would say, No, John, not now. You're building big time. Keep doing what you're doing. Don't confuse the readers. If you ever get really, really big, maybe we'll let you do one off-brand book (and so he did become really, really big and published *A Painted House*).

So . . . if you want to build a money-making career publishing e-books, you need to think about your brand as you get started. What sort of book do you want to write most? Will your readers be able to follow you from book to book with similar expectations?

If you want to write more than one kind of book, you need to consider how the marketplace will perceive it. One way to do that is to use a pseudonym for another genre of book. Nora Roberts uses J. D. Robb, for example.

These are the sorts of long term plans you need to spend time on, because once you get rolling, if potential readers are confused, you may never get established.

But here is the most important question of all:

Can you deliver a great reading experience each and every time?

That's the subject of the following section.

Just Because You Wrote It Doesn't Mean You Should Publish It

This morning, all over this fabled land of ours, a legion of previously unpublished and rejected writers-in-waiting awoke, smiled, jumped out of bed and shot to their computers, sat down and shouted, "Power to the people, baby!" and took up once again where they had left off yesterday, uploading self-published fiction to the Internet.

Some of this content might even be readable. However, a great deal of it will consist of 50,000 or more words of hideous prose, stilted dialogue and a plot that has about as much cohesion as a Joe Biden press conference.

Yet all will be accompanied by thoughts of, "I don't need no steenkin' publisher!"

Self-publishing used to have a built-in de-motivator: money. You had to pony up to get into print. Either you paid an outlandish sum to a vanity press, or you figured out a way to typeset your book and get it printed in bulk, leading to that sure sign of the self-published author: the garage filled with boxes of books.

Now, with e-publishing, printing is no longer an issue. Even so, with print-on-demand (POD), you can still render a paper book without having to print and warehouse a ton of them.

So it is now possible for you to publish painlessly. But just because you wrote it doesn't mean you should.

Now, I'm not against the American dream, freedom of the press, or the writer-as-rebel. Goodness knows there is a grand tradition here, from Whitman and Twain right up to Joe Konrath (who made a big splash in 2010 with his exclusive deal to publish with Amazon).

But step back a moment and consider whether you want to jump in too soon.

The Konrath deal is unique. He has a track record of traditionally published books, a fan base and a popular blog. For him, the deal makes sense. But the bottom line (at least as far as I am concerned) is that *he knows the craft of writing fiction.*

Do you? You may think you do. But just because you wrote it doesn't mean you know it. And if you throw your work up to the Kindle store, perhaps in the hopes a traditional publisher will take notice, you could actually be harming your long term prospects.

You may not care. Perhaps you think you'll reap that sweet 70% royalty on a $2.99 book forever, and pull down six figures like Konrath is doing.

Well, you won't, unless a) you know how to get noticed; b) your book is good enough to generate word of mouth; and c) you write more and more books that are as good or better.

But learning to write books like that takes time. Lots of time.

Okay, let's say you've put that in. You've been working at this craft for years. You've been critique-grouped to death. You've got that in-box full of rejections. By thunder, you're not going to take it anymore!

I implore you, before you hit the upload button, do the following:

1. Get your manuscript to five "beta" readers. These should be people who are not just going to gush over your work, but people you can trust to give you direct comments on likes and dislikes. Make sure 4 out of 5 give it high marks, and the fifth is pretty close.

Note: this is not your critique group (if you're in one). Such groups have their own peculiar dynamics. What you want are people who will experience the book as the average reader would.

Be patient. Buy them lunch or send them a Starbucks card for their trouble. Talk to them and get them to give you detailed feedback.

2. Hire a freelance editor. It's well worth it find somebody who can go over the manuscript, catch glaring errors, and offer fixes. Do your research, though, and make sure you get what you pay for.

3. Pay for a good cover design. Nothing looks cheesier than a typical, self-pubbed, self-designed cover. I recently went browsing at the Kindle store, looking at self-published works. The covers were, by and large, terrible. Unless you have strong graphic and artistic ability, find a way to get a great cover.

4. Even after your upload, do not get overconfident. The odds are stacked against you making any significant money this way. But if you want to be a real writer, and not just somebody who has made a book available, keep growing and working at the craft.

The modern self-publishing movement, which began with Bill Henderson's *The Publish-it-Yourself Handbook* (1973) has just taken a quantum leap forward with e-publishing. But the same caveat that applied then applies now: just because you wrote it doesn't mean it's ready.

Be patient. Take some time. Don't go it completely alone.

Then, if you want to play, go ahead. You're still free to try your hand at this. As Henderson wrote back in '73: "Publishing-it-yourself is in the individualistic tradition of the American dream."

Just do your dreaming with your eyes wide open.

Act Like a Professional

I've been teaching at writers conferences for over fifteen years, and I've seen a ton of aspiring writers in various stages of disequilibrium. Everyone wants to get a book contract, and everyone's a little scared they never will. They hear stories about the odds and it sends shivers to the tips of their typing fingers.

Those who persevere have a chance.

In the course of these conference years I've seen a number of writers who have gotten that contract and gone on to be published by major houses. I've even helped a few get there, which is nice. And while it's nearly impossible to judge why one manuscript makes it and another, which is comparable or even better, does not, I have made note of one item. The overwhelming majority of writers I've seen make it are those who look and act like a professional.

When you meet unpublished writers who act like pros, you form the immediate impression that it's only a matter of time before they make it. This impression is not lost on agents and editors.

So what are the marks of a professional?

1. Grooming. Successful writers-in-waiting *look* professional. They do not come off as slobs or slackers. They dress sharply though unpretentiously. They say you can't judge a book by its cover, but we do it all the time with people. Don't shoot down your first impression by looking unkempt or having stink-breath that can kill low flying birds.

2. Industry knowledge. Professionals know something about their profession. They spend time reading blogs and books and the trades, though not to the exclusion of their writing.

3. To the point. A pro has the ability to focus on what the other person (e.g., an agent) will find valuable and, most important, can deliver that in a concise and persuasive manner. You should be able to tell someone, in 30 seconds or less, what your book is about, in such a way that the person can immediately see its potential.

4. Courtesy. Common courtesy goes a long way. If you have an appointment with an agent, be there two minutes early. When you're done, thank them. Follow up with a short and appropriate e-mail. Don't call them unless you've been invited to. Don't get angry or petulant, even if there's a reason for it. Burning bridges is never a good career move.

5. Take action every day. Over the long haul, a successful professional in any field is always in a growth mode. Always looking for ways to improve, studying, doing, taking action toward goals. When you do this, day after day, you begin to build momentum. That, in turn, will fuel your confidence and keep you going. And there is nothing an unpublished writer needs more than motivation to keep going.

So . . . keep writing. Keep learning. And act like a pro.

The Writing Life

Some of My Favorite Writing Quotes

Here fore your consideration are seven quotes on the writing life. Do you collect writer quotes? You should. They can be inspirational and instructive.

"You must stay drunk on writing so reality cannot destroy you." – **Ray Bradbury**

Source: *Zen in the Art of Writing* by Ray Bradbury

"Do not look toward writing as a profession. Work at something else. Dig ditches if you have to, but keep writing in the status of a hobby that you can work at in your spare time. Writing, to me, is a hobby — by trade I'm a farmer." – **William Faulkner**

Source: *On Being a Writer* (1989, Writer's Digest Books, ed. Bill Strickland)

"When I was younger and first beginning to write, I'd think I was going to get the Pulitzer and the Booker and the Nobel Prize. Now I don't give a damn. I'm content to know that I write . . . *good.* I'm a good writer and that's all I care about." – Evan Hunter (aka Ed McBain)

Source: Writer's Digest, Sept. 1996

"I think that the difference right now between good art and bad art is that the good artists are the people who are, in one way or another, creating, out of deep and honest concern, a vision of life . . . that is worth living. And the bad artists, of whom there are many, are whining or moaning or staring, because it's fashionable, into the dark abyss." – John Gardner

Source: *The Writer's Chapbook* (1989, Penguin, ed. George Plimpton)

"You must avoid giving hostages to fortune, like getting an expensive wife, an expensive house, and a style of living that never lets you afford the time to take the chance to write what you wish." – Irwin Shaw

Source: *Writers on Writing* (1990, Running Press, ed. John Winokur)

"If you want to write fiction, the best thing you can do is take two aspirins, lie down in a dark room, and wait for the feeling to pass. If the feeling persists, you probably ought to write a novel." – Lawrence Block

Source: *Writing the Novel* (1979, Writer's Digest Books)

"I write to entertain. In a world that encompasses so much pain and fear and cruelty, it is noble to provide a few hours of escape, moments of delight and forgetfulness." - Dean Koontz

Source: *How to Write Best Selling Fiction* (1981, Writer's Digest Books)

My Personal Writing Routine

I'm sometimes asked what my daily writing routine looks like, so here it is:

My day starts early. I get up while it's still nice and dark and start the coffee brewing. I have a quiet time -- a personal spiritual exercise -- then I hop on the Internet for news and blogs and some email. I usually get to my writing desk around 6 or 6:30.

First order of business is to prioritize my writing day. I always have a list of projects, and stack them according to their importance. Obviously, if I'm on a tight deadline, that project will be at the top. But I've also planned out my writing a year in advance, so I always have more than one thing to work on.

I'll take a look at my previous day's writing and clean up obvious errors, make things clearer, touch up the style. No major revisions, though. I do my major edits after a draft is done.

Then I'm off to the races, as it were. I have a weekly quota of words to do. This is, I think, the most important practice of all for a writer. You have to produce the words. Doing that makes you a better writer, teaches you discipline, and eventually adds up to a book. Then, over the course of time, many books.

I aim for a daily quota, but know there are just some days where things happen and I can't write. By keeping focused on a weekly count, though, I can adjust. I aim for a thousand words each day, but if I miss a day I know I can make it up tomorrow.

I also take one day off from writing each week, Sunday. This recharges my batteries and makes Monday more productive.

I try to get my daily quota in as early as possible. It makes the rest of the day go more smoothly. I'll write in my office at home, or pack up and go to Starbucks. Sometimes I like to have a little activity going on around me. But if some kid has the screaming mimi's, or there's a particularly loud conversation going on at the table next to mine, I'll pop on the Bose headphones and listen to movie soundtracks as I write.

Coffee, of course, is a given. But I don't overdo it. I don't want to end up like Balzac, who drank dozens of cups of thick, black tar each day. He was convinced of its magical effects on the imagination and the speed of his writing, but he died of caffeine poisoning at fifty-one.

I try to write when I'm not writing, too. I carry around a little notebook, so when ideas occur to me I can jot them down. Or I'll do a voice memo on my phone so I don't forget something. This causes me to get a far off look sometimes, even if I'm in a conversation with someone. It's a curse of the writing life.

I also use the AlphaSmart Neo for quick writing stints in odd places.

If I'm editing a draft, I'll have a file folder or notebook of pages with me. I do that work only after I've done my writing quota.

Now, I well understand most people don't have total flexibility for their writing. There are full time jobs, family obligations, maybe health challenges. But I do believe everyone can get in a weekly quota of words. How many words varies. My advice is to set a realistic goal, one you know you can reach, and then up it by 10%. Make that number what you go for.

Maybe there's only one day a week when you can write for a length of time without interruption. Plan accordingly. You'll be pleased when you look up six months from now and see a book, or most of a book, completed.

That's pretty much all there is to it. I look at my writing for what it is, my job. I get up every day and go to work. I try to do my best with every page. Then I clock out.

Consider Your Worth: Your Personal Writing Schedule

1. Look at your week on a planning calendar. Your electronic calendar or one you buy from the store. Shade in all the times that are absolute in your week. Your job, for example. Get a picture of where your time actually goes.

2. Find blanks in your calendar and make writing appointments. Do this every week.

3. At the beginning of your week, look at the time you have, and set a word goal. If you don't know what that should be, start with 300 words an hour. Do that loyally and see how it feels. If you make it comfortably, raise the quota. Find that spot that's just a little bit of a challenge.

4. Now stick to this schedule religiously. Revise it every six months or so until you are a lean, mean producing machine. That's really the basic discipline of the writing life. All else is secondary.

Is the Outlook for Fiction Bleak?

Whenever I find myself growing grim about the mouth; whenever it is a damp, drizzly November in my soul; whenever I find myself involuntarily pausing before coffin warehouses, and bringing up the rear of every funeral I meet; and especially whenever my hypos get such an upper hand of me, that it requires a strong moral principle to prevent me from deliberately stepping into the street, and methodically knocking people's hats off--then, I account it high time to get to sea as soon as I can. This is my substitute for pistol and ball. - Moby-Dick

November, 2009, felt like the month the Earth stood still. Or imploded. Or got hit by that tsunami in the movie *2012*.

It seemed like that month all the upheavals in the publishing industry started to coalesce into one big flaming mess on the order of the Hindenburg. At least, that's how it sounded on various blogs and comment sections, where rhetoric sometimes reached conflagration levels.

All the anxiety over eBooks and eReaders, the move of some big publishers into the self-publishing market, the revelation of paltry incomes associated even with a *New York Times* bestselling book, and the apprehension of authors and agents over just how anybody is going make any kind of a buck as a novelist anymore – it all seemed to come to a head that bleak November.

Why was this so?

First, the very pace of change in our world is now such that major developments happen almost as fast as chair throwing incidents on *Jerry Springer.* And humans naturally feel anxious about change until we can catch up and figure out what's going on. But we always seem to feel a few steps behind these days.

Technological changes seem poised to alter the paradigms we've lived with for centuries, such as books on paper being paid for by readers. No one knows what a paradigm shift feels like until they've actually been through it, and we haven't been *through* it yet. We're *inside* it.

The only thing we know for certain is nothing is certain, and the landscape we see today will be very different tomorrow.

I have but two predictions:

1. People are still going to want good stories to read.

2. They're not going to pay as much money to get them.

As to #1, writers need to do what they've always done: write and write well. Over and over. That calls for commitment to the craft and resistance to the "easy way" of self-publishing.

Let's be blunt. We all know the overwhelming majority of self-published books aren't good enough to be published the traditional way. That doesn't mean there aren't exceptions. There are. But they are as rare as Susan Boyle.

Yes, I do believe authors will do more direct selling in the future. They will make their stuff available in digital form directly. But they still have to prove themselves to be good writers, or people won't buy.

Which leads to #2. Consumers are being trained to pay $10 or less for books. This means hardcovers are probably a dinosaur. The mastodons are in the tar pits.

But there will still be a market for books, because of #1. You know what it feels like? The mass market paperback boom post-World War II. Low price point, ease of use. The eBook revolution may be recreating this type of market.

The cream will rise to the top. Those novelists who can deliver, book after book, are going to gain a following and have the chance to make some coin.

So whenever I get to feeling like old Ishmael, with a "damp, drizzly November of the soul," and when I, too, want to go outside and knock some hats off, I remember that fiction writers will always be around. The world needs us.

Maybe now more than ever.

Consider Your Worth: Fighting That November

1. If you ever catch yourself feeling bleak about the writing business, your prospects, or anything else relating to the world of books and stories, start writing.

2. Write for ten minutes without stopping. Let the ideas and words flow. Follow where they lead. Maybe you're continuing a novel, or maybe you're making a new one up. Maybe you make up a character and write a scene, or maybe you just want to vent. Whatever it is, writing itself forces out the drizzly November of the soul.

3. Repeat as necessary.

Stay Thirsty

I love a good ad campaign.

When I started running a small legal publishing business years ago, I had to teach myself advertising and marketing. I read some classics on the subject, such as *How to Write a Good Advertisement* by Victor O. Schwab and *Tested Advertising Methods* by John Caples.

My favorite, though, was *Ogilvy on Advertising* by the legendary ad man David Ogilvy. This volume made me appreciate what goes into successful ads, and just how hard they are to pull off.

So when I see a great ad campaign, I nod in approval. One of the best of all time has to be the "I'm a Mac, I'm a PC" series. It's no accident that Mac's market share has shot up in tandem with these ads. Smart, funny, short, well acted, superb.

My current favorite is "The most interesting man in the world" campaign for Dos Equis.

A typical spot features "vintage film" of the man in various pursuits, while a narrator recites a few facts about him. Then we see him sitting in a bar surrounded by beautiful people. He looks into the camera and, in a slight Spanish accent, says, "I don't always drink beer, but when I do I prefer Dos Equis."

A few of my favorite "facts" about this man are:

He lives vicariously through himself.

He once had an awkward moment, just to see how it feels.

The police often question him, just because they find him interesting.

He once taught a German shepherd to bark in Spanish.

And then, at the end of each ad, comes the man's signature sign off: "Stay thirsty, my friends."

What's so good about this campaign?

It's risky. Having a graying, middle aged man as the lead character is, as they say, counter programming.

It's funny without trying too hard. The understated way the deep-voiced narrator extols the man's legend is pitch perfect.

It has a complete backstory, revealed a little at a time in the mock film clips.

These are qualities of a good novel, too. Risky, in that it doesn't repeat the same old; a bit of unforced humor is always welcome; and a backstory that renders characters real and complex without slowing down the narrative. All that we can learn from "the most interesting man in the world" campaign.

And from the man himself we can learn, as writers, to live life expansively and not just lollygag through our existence. Not waiting for inspiration but going after it, as Jack London once said, "with a club." Believing, with Kerouac, in the "holy contour of life."

We ought to be seekers as well as storytellers, a little mad sometimes, risking the pity and scorn of our fellows as we pursue the artistic vision. Then we park ourselves at the keyboard and strive to get it down on the page. Why go through it all? Because the world needs dreams rendered in words.

Writer, keep after it and someday this may be said of you as well: "His charisma can be seen from space. Even his enemies list him as their emergency contact number."

Stay thirsty, my friends.

Consider Your Worth: Are You Thirsty?

1. Ask yourself this question: if you knew the odds against you being published were a million to one, would you continue to write? Can you believe that you can change the odds by getting better, and that you will if you keep trying?

2. How are you living life "expansively"? What risks do you need to take, especially in your writing, to get "further"?

Driving Dangerously

Among the stranger headlines I've ever seen is the following:

Man Driving with Snakes in His Pants Causes Multi-car Accident

According to one online source:

A man in Hartford, Connecticut caused a multi-car crash

after he claimed two pet baby snakes escaped from his pants pockets . . .

Angel Rolon, 20, told police he lost control of his SUV when the snakes slithered near the gas and brake pedals. Rolon said as he and his passenger tried to catch them, the SUV veered into some parked cars and overturned.

Animal control officers at the scene were unable to locate the snakes, and police have not confirmed Rolon's story.

Rolon was treated at a hospital for unknown injuries. Police say they gave him a summons for reckless driving and other charges.

Now as I recall, my dad told me never to drive with alcohol in my blood or snakes in my pants. He was very emphatic about that. Doesn't every kid learn this valuable lesson before taking the family car out for a spin?

"Remember, son, no drag racing and no legless reptiles in your Levis. Have you got that?"

"Yes, sir."

"If you have *any* ectothermic squamate in your jeans while you're behind the wheel, you're grounded."

"I understand, sir."

In all candor, though, I must admit there is an application for fiction writers here. You see, writing a full length novel is very much like driving a car with snakes in your pants-- you just never know what's going to happen. You may start out with great intentions, but somewhere along the way some major slithering will take place. You may feel prepared to handle any eventuality, but when reptiles are loose around the gas pedal you could end up in a major collision.

We all set off on our "drive" to write with some trepidation, knowing there will be inevitable setbacks, disappointments, even book-ending accidents. But that doesn't stop us, if we really have the chops, the desire. You want to write, you write, snakes or no.

Consider Your Worth: Write the Next Page

Next time you're feeling those snakes all around you, put your head down and write *the next page*. That's all. One page. You'll find there will be fewer snakes left when you're done.

Hanging Upside Down and Other Creative Moves

September, 2009, was Dan Brown week in the world of publishing. And that was a good thing. The business needed a shot in the arm. We needed to see hardcovers flying off the shelves again. We needed people sitting around Starbucks talking fiction, getting caught up in a story world.

There was a lot of chatter about the phenomenon of *The Lost Symbol*, as there was for *The Da Vinci Code*. But here I'd like to focus on another aspect of this event: the author himself.

The Lost Symbol was not easy for Mr. Brown. I mean, how do you follow a once-in-a-lifetime hit like *TDVC*? That book's particular mix of vast religious conspiracy, symbology and fast paced action, went spinning around on the wheel of fortune and hit the jackpot.

Brown copped to the pressure of following up. Regarding the long lag time between *TDVC* and *The Lost Symbol*, Dan Brown was quoted in the *L.A. Times* as follows:

"The thing that happened to me and must happen to any writer who's had success is that I temporarily became very self-aware. Instead of writing and saying, 'This is what the character does,' you say, 'Wait, millions of people are going to read this.' ... You're temporarily crippled....[later] The furor died down, and I realized that none of it had any relevance to what I was doing. I'm just a guy who tells a story."

Writers, attend to this. What happened to Dan Brown on a mega level happens to most writers who publish more than one book. A lot of unpublished writers think things will be just swell once they're published, and they can produce book after book with nary a worry.

The truth is, writing fiction gets harder because we continue to raise the bar on ourselves. We do, that is, if we truly care about the craft. We know more about what we do with each book, and where we fall short. We hope we have a growing readership, and want to keep pleasing them, surprising them, delighting them with plot twists, great characters and a bit of stylistic flair.

But we can't stroll down the aisle of "Plots R Us" and choose something fresh, right out of the box. (Although Erle Stanley Gardner was known to use a complex "plot wheel." I guess he did okay). We are on a never ending quest for premises, characters and plot. No matter how many books we've done, we keep aspiring to the next level.

Dan Brown reportedly deals with all this by using gravity shoes. He hangs upside down, letting the blood rush to his head. Bats use the same method. But there are other options.

Whenever you are wondering if you've got the stuff to be published (or, if published, to stay that way), let me offer a few helps.

1. Write. This is the most important thing of all. Get "black on white," as Maupassant used to say. Even if you feel like pond scum as an artist, just start writing. If you can't possibly face a page of your project, write a free form journal about something in your past. Begin with "I remember . . ." Pretty soon, you'll feel like getting back to your novel.

2. Re-read. Pull out a favorite novel, one that really moved you. Read parts of it at random, or even the whole thing. Don't worry about feeling even worse because you think you can't write like that author. You're not supposed to. You never can. But guess what? He can't write like you, either.

3. Incubate. For half an hour think hard about your project, writing notes to yourself, asking questions. Back yourself into tight corners. Then put all that away for a day and do something else. Walk. Swim. Work your day job. Stuff will be bubbling in your "writer's brain." The next day, write.

4. Turn off your Internet browser for a whole day. By which I mean, of course, first read The Kill Zone, then turn off the Net and write. Forget emails, Twitter, Facebook, MySpace, or anybody else's space. A bit of downtime from all the noise is good for focus.

Mental landmines abound for writers. The key is not to let any of them stop you from writing, even if you have to hang upside down to do it.

Will Arrogance Get You Published?

Let's talk about arrogance. Because I say so.

We've all noticed an uptick in the arrogance factor in society. *New York Times* opinion writer David Brooks wrote in a 2009 column:

When you look from today back to 1945, you are looking into a different cultural epoch, across a sort of narcissism line. Humility, the sense that nobody is that different from anybody else, was a large part of the culture then. But that humility came under attack in the ensuing decades. Self-effacement became identified with conformity and self-repression. A different ethos came to the fore, which the sociologists call "expressive individualism."

Now, in one sense, "expressive individualism" is what we do as writers. We are boldly sharing part of ourselves, and should do so confidently. But here's the thing: *this confidence should be evident in our pages alone.* When it's off the page and in people's faces, "expressive individualism" can too easily become slap-deserving arrogance.

There are so many examples of such arrogance in culture. One of the most notable was Kanye West deciding he could interrupt Taylor Swift's acceptance speech at the 2009 MTV VMA awards. Taking Swift's microphone, and moment, West extolled the merits of another nominee in front of a national television audience. Why? Because of "expressive individualism" gone awry.

So the idea that *it's all about me and I will make you admit it* is part of the *zeitgeist,* just another move you make to get what you want.

And it's filtering down like an acid drip into the world of aspiring writers. When I speak at writers conferences I am gratified that most people seem eager to learn and determined to grow. But there has been an increase in those who think that having a chip on their shoulders is an essential part of their campaign to get published.

It's isn't.

True, there are some people who *are* arrogant and who *do* get published. But they get published in spite of their arrogance, not because of it. They get published because they can actually write.

But for the large majority of the new arroganti, such behavior is not going to get them closer to a contract. It will, in fact, hinder their chances.

Confidence, on the other hand, is good. And necessary. But there is a fine line between confidence and arrogance. That line is something called *professionalism*.

A professional doesn't waste another person's time by overstaying his welcome.

A professional knows what someone – i.e., an agent or editor – is looking for, and delivers it in a precise manner.

A professional doesn't follow up frustrations with nasty notes, diatribes, or slanderous blog posts. Nor tear down other writers who get published.

In other words, a true professional knows when to put a cork in it and get back to the business of learning to write better.

A professional will, over time, gain respect, even when rejected. That leaves doors open for future submissions. The arrogant burn bridges and find doors slamming.

Arrogance talks smack. Confidence does its talking on the page.

So be bold, be confident, be "expressively individualistic," but use that energy for the writing itself. Instead of thinking up ways to offend people, commit to doing something to become a better writer, every day.

Because even if you succeed while being arrogant, even if you land on the bestseller list, it will be a Pyrrhic victory. As writer Michael Bishop puts it, "One may achieve remarkable writerly success while flunking all the major criteria for success as a human being. Try not to do that."

Consider Your Worth: Is there a chip on your shoulder?
Be honest about it. Are you in love with your arrogance? Do you think it's essential for your happiness? Do you see lack of arrogance as "weakness"? Do a little cognitive therapy on yourself. Think it through. And if, at the end, you still decide to be cocky, figure out a way to translate that into energy for your writing and determine to do as little damage to your personal and professional relationships as possible.

Envy

Years ago there was a commercial for Pepto-Bismol, where a nerdy guy in glasses looked straight into the camera and said something like, "Can we talk about diarrhea?" It was an effective ad because, well, they took the bull by the horns, as it were. They didn't sugar coat the malady; they didn't try to cleverly talk around it.

People get diarrhea. They don't like to talk about it, but sometimes they have to in order to stop it.

That's the feeling I have right now in talking to writers about a malady that may affect every one of them from time to time: envy. Can we talk?

Ann Lamott has a great chapter on envy in her writing book, *Bird by Bird*. Here, in part, is what she says:

If you continue to write, you are probably going to have to deal with it because some wonderful, dazzling successes are going to happen for some of the most awful, angry, undeserving writers you know—people who are, in other words, not you. You are going to feel awful beyond words. you are going to have a number of days in a row where you hate everyone and don't believe in anything . . . If you do know the author whose turn it is, he or she will inevitably say that it will be your turn next, which is what the bride always says to you at each successive wedding, while you grow older and more decayed . . . It can wreak just the tiniest bit of havoc with your self-esteem to find that you are hoping for small bad things to happen to this friend—for, say, her head to blow up.

Funny, yes; but the truth is that envy is a serious waste of time and a drain on your energy. Like any emotion, it can be a chronic condition or a momentary blip. If it is the former, you really have to do something to eradicate it. Let me suggest a few things:

1. Acknowledge your humanity and the fact that you care about what you're doing. That's the basic reason you feel the way you do. You're invested in your writing emotionally, as you should be. You're also not perfect, and don't expect you ever will be.

2. Look at the part of your feelings that wants the other person to fail, or not enjoy success. That's the ugly bit you've got to get rid of. If you have an active spiritual life, this is a good place to bring out the big guns. The Book of Proverbs, chapter 14, verse 30 says, "A heart at peace gives life to the body, but envy rots the bones." The ancient philosopher Epicurus wrote: "Do not spoil what you have by desiring what you have not; remember that what you now have was once among the things you only hoped for." Whatever practice you engage in, the great religions and spiritual views have always talked about the jewel of *contentment.* Buddha said, "Health is the greatest gift, contentment the greatest wealth." That's worth pursuing.

3. Write. This is always the best antidote to any writerly anxiety. Get involved in your project. Put your head down and produce the words.

4. Improve. Anyone – *anyone* – can improve their craft. You are always at a certain level, and you can with some effort get to the next level. Your competition is really only with yourself. There is joy and confidence when you see yourself improving.

5. Prepare. Know that a pang of envy may come at any time. Before that happens, affirm your own worth and say a bit of Lawrence Block's "A Writer's Prayer" (from his book, *Telling Lies for Fun and Profit):*

For starters, help me to avoid comparing myself to other writers. I can make a lot of trouble for myself when I do that . . .Lord, help me remember that I'm not in competition with other writers. Whether they have more or less success has nothing to do with me. They have their stories to write and I have mine. They have their way of writing them and I have mine. They have their careers and

I have mine. The more focus on comparing myself with them, the less energy I am able to concentrate on making the best of myself and my own work. I wind up despairing of my ability and bitter about its fruits, and all I manage to do is sabotage myself...When I read a writer who does things better than I do, enable me to learn from him...

A hearty Amen to that.

Consider Your Worth: Turn Envy to Energy

The next time you feel envious:

1. Own it. Don't wish it away. You feel it. That's the way it is.

2. Write something. Anything. Work on a project, or make notes for a new one, or just do a 10 minute writing-without-stopping exercise.

3. And speaking of exercise, exercise. Turn envy into energy for writing, and into physical activity.

A Sense of Where You Are

I've been playing basketball most of my life. When I was a kid, falling in love with the game, I happened across a book called *A Sense of Where You Are* by John McPhee. It was a profile of Bill Bradley when he was one of the best college hoopsters ever, nearly leading lowly Princeton to the national title.

What impressed me was Bradley's work ethic. He practiced for hours a day, in all sorts of weather, perfecting his shots, his moves. He even spent considerable time on the classic hook shot, in order to have a complete game.

So the summer between seventh and eighth grade I had my dad put up a basket on our driveway. I practiced every day, sometimes in the rain, sometimes into the night with the driveway lit up by a single floodlight.

I got books on basketball technique from the library and taught myself the proper way to shoot a jump shot. I learned you have to keep your elbow in, not flared out. I learned to give the ball a perfect spin. In fact, I became the deadliest shot in the history of Parkman Junior High School. In further fact, I was All League in high school and played a year in college. In furthest fact, had I been a couple inches taller and about five seconds faster, I'd be in the Basketball Hall of Fame.

Larry Bird? Pheh.

But I digress.

The other morning, as is my wont, I was shooting around a local park when I got into doing some hook shots. Now that's one shot I worked on a little bit when I was younger, but never really developed into something deadly. My specialty was the 15 - 20 foot jumper, and that's what I practiced most.

But this day, for some reason, it occurred to me that as I had taught myself the proper way to shoot a jump shot, maybe I ought to take another look at the hook. So I started to experiment with a different release point, looking for another feel. And in about five minutes I happened on a slightly modified shot, but that modification made a huge difference. The hooks started to fall.

I felt like a kid again, with the joy of discovering a new technique that works. After all these years, I had a stronger hook shot with only a few adjustments.

I bring this up because I get this feeling as a writer, too. I still get excited when I put a new spin on a technique and it works. That's why I continue to read books on writing, *Writer's Digest* magazine, blogs and lots and lots of novels, seeing what works, trying stuff out. My philosophy is if I learn just one thing, or get a new view on something I already know, it's worth it.

Don't ever think you have arrived. When you think that, even if you're multi-published, you start to atrophy. There are authors who once cared about the craft but now just mail it in, because they have an established following.

Don't let that be you. Respect the craft, and keep at it.

In his book, McPhee described Bill Bradley's ability to throw up a shot with his back to the basket – no look – and make it most of the time. When he asked Bradley how he could do that, Bradley replied, "You develop a sense of where you are."

Know where you are, writer, and how you can get better. Then practice. That's really the secret to succeeding as a writer. Maybe the only secret: practice -- day after week after year.

Consider Your Worth: Be Purposeful in Improvement

1. Take an hour and write yourself a letter. Tell yourself what you think of you as a writer. Be honest.

2. Identify "weak spots" in your writing by referring to the letter. Turn those areas into a list.

3. Attack that list by reading writing books that cover that

subject. Study. Practice. Grow.

Courage to Write

It takes courage to write.

Not the kind of courage that a soldier displays going into battle, or a firefighter reveals charging into a burning building. That's elevated courage, the kind that deserves to be honored in our culture. I'm not getting anywhere near to describing that kind of guts.

I'm talking about the non-lethal world, where it takes a degree of courage to do almost anything worth doing. Because for every enterprise of note there are critics and doubters, scoffers and jeerers, ready to pour acid rain on your parade.

It takes courage to write because obstacles and doubts come in many forms and build big brick walls to try to stop your progress.

Dick Simon (of Simon & Schuster) once said, "All writers are scared to death. Some simply hide it better than others."

We all know the publishing business is in major shakeup mode right now. Trying to predict the future of the industry is sort of like trying to judge the family prospects of guests on *Jerry Springer* — can any relationship survive?

With all this going on, any writer – new or established – can start to wonder: Is the dream worth it? Do I have any chance of getting published? Staying published? Am I good enough? Am I a fraud? Are the odds too great?

Every true writer faces questions like this. And every true

writer finds a way to dig down and write on.

As a professional writer (and even before publication) I've faced all the same doubts. Through trial and error I worked out a few ways to keep on keeping on. Maybe one of these will help next time you feel like throwing in the towel.

1. Think in terms of *one more page*. Don't ponder the future or replay the past. Don't stew about the industry or the myriad things you can't control. Think about the work in front of you. Get that page done, then move on to the next. Establish a quota system and stick to it. The writing itself becomes the best way out of the bog of doubt.

2. Get some visual motivation. When I decided I was going to be a writer no matter what, I went out and bought a black coffee mug with *Writer* written in gold across it. A little corny, sure, but I didn't care. I wanted to earn the right to be called a writer, and seeing the cup daily reminded me of the commitment I'd made.

In my office now I have pictures of three writers I admire.

The first is of Stephen King, in his home office, feet up on the desk, looking over a manuscript. He's dressed casually. His dog is under his legs, looking at the camera.

This is my idea of the good life.

Then there's a picture of John D. MacDonald, tapping away at his typewriter, pipe in mouth. He was prolific (his biography is entitled *Red Hot Typewriter*) and a master of story and style.

The photo reminds me to keep producing words.

Finally, I have a picture of Evan Hunter/Ed McBain, from the back of one of his novels, arms folded, staring out as if in challenge. He was even more prolific than MacDonald, writing both literary and genre novels.

If I'm not working hard enough, his glare reminds me to get going again.

3. Go to a bookstore and browse. Look at author photos and dust jackets. See what's come out lately. If you can, make it an independent bookstore, and *buy a book from them*. They are folks who love books and are struggling mightily right now. Show a little support, then go back to your keyboard and write.

4. Re-read some favorites. I have a shelf of novels I especially love. Sometimes I'll take one down at random and start reading. I get inspired again with the pure joy of what writing can be. Then I try to make some magic happen on my own page.

5. Remember what Satchel Paige once said: "Don't look back. Something may be gaining on you."

About Platforms

What is a platform? It comes from the world of public speaking. It's something you stand on so you can yak at people. A lot of people.

Metaphorically, if you have a lot of people listening to you, you have a platform. And publishers like that because it means many of those people may buy your book.

Sounds simple. But platforms for fiction writers may have a trap door. We'd best talk about it so you don't fall through.

We have to distinguish between non-fiction and fiction. Non-fiction writers who specialize in a subject, or are known for something they've done, have a natural platform, namely all the people who are into the subject matter or celebrity thing.

So Suzie Orman, a recognized financial expert, can sell books because of her expertise. She can speak, and people who want financial advice will come and listen. At the back of the room her staff can sell books and DVDs. It's a money making operation.

Not so the fiction writer. We write stories intended to reach a diverse readership, which translates into: people who are hard to find.

The Internet seemed to be the way to handle that challenge. After all, a billion people use the Internet. All we have to do is set up a blog about our books, and we have a billion potential hits! Wow! Get just one percent to buy your novel (and they will, because of that snazzy book trailer!) and you've sold ten million books!

Of course, that was fifteen years ago in a dream. The reality is that in the flurry of Internet fog it's hard to get any attention at all. And even if you do (here it comes, the takeaway): That does not guarantee a fiction writing career for you.

As writer Simon Wood recently put it:

"There's a massive pinball effect with a writer's work. Someone reads a story and likes it, so they check out something else I've written. That only works if what is out there is good. If it's bad, it has the converse effect

and they're unlikely to seek out other works."

Writers have simply got to understand it's not pervasive marketing that sells *over the long term*, but the stories themselves. You can market yourself to an *introduction*, but the readers will base future purchases on how much they like what they read, not on how many titles you have available on the Internet in digital form, or how many Twitter followers you've collared.

Unpublished fiction writers need to quit obsessing over platform, quit re-designing fancy websites, quit posting first chapters on Facebook, quit trying to jump start careers via Twitter. What they need to be concentrating on is *writing a book readers can't put down*--can't put down because the writer has spent years bleeding desire and passion and is unashamedly putting that on the page, using all the tools of the craft learned bit by painful bit by writing every day.

When you write books readers love, platform takes care of itself, because word-of-mouth and repeat readership are the only two planks that count.

Am I saying don't do any of this Internet or social networking stuff? Of course not. I do some of it. It's out there and you have choices. What I am saying is this:

Do what you can in the marketing/promotion matrix without:

1. Harming the quality of your writing;

2. Harming the quality of your family and personal relationships; and

3. Going into debt.

Follow those guidelines and write your best stuff. Doing so will drain all the anxiety out of the word *platform*.

[After this post appeared, I received some comments. One or two suggested it was "easy for me to say" being an established writer who has a platform, and had one at the start. Another suggested it all seems like a "Catch-22." Below is what I replied.]

Yes, it seems like a "Catch-22" but I think it's more like a "Catch-1 1/2." A "fiction writing platform" *before* publication seems rather like a cart before the horse item, and it will take one HUGE platform (on the order of mini-celebrity) to overcome the hurdle of a story that's not ready for prime time. OTOH, I don't know any publisher who will not jump on a new novel they think will catch on with readers, just because the writer doesn't have 5,000 Twitter followers. If such exists, the term "short sighted" comes to mind.

When I started writing, the word platform was unheard of (just like I was). I built up my readership over the course of years, concentrating always on getting better as a writer, book after book. Any platform I have now is more the result, not the cause, of whatever success I've had as a writer. My main thing is for the new writer not to stress over platform. Do what you can, like I said, but don't ever let it take away from the writing itself.

Consider Your Worth: Avoiding Platform Fever

1. On a stress scale from 1 – 10, 1 being virtually comatose and 10 so stressed your head might explode, where are you? Take a moment and jot the number down.

2. If you are at 6 or above, you need to scale back by

becoming more objective about your self-promotion efforts. Write a letter to yourself, as if you were an outside consultant, explaining your current situation, followed by a recommendation that you do *less* for a period of time.

3. If you are between 2 and 5, that's not a bad place. Create a plan to keep doing what you are doing, but in a way that does not hurt your writing. A regular but time-sensitive schedule is to be preferred. For example, you could limit your Twitter feeds to fifteen minutes, total, per day.

10 Things You Need to Know About Agents

1. Before you approach an agent, make sure your concept is killer. That means a) not shopworn ("We've seen this before"); or b) not so far off the map that anyone with a profit motive will run screaming from the room. It has to be fresh but not too weird. The characters have to jump off the page. There has to be enough at stake. Your opening pages have too move. Easy, right? Of course not, because if it was your Aunt Sally would be writing *New York Times* bestsellers. But here's where you have to dig in if you want to interest and agent.

2. You are better off having no agent than having a bad agent. Anyone can print up business cards and call themselves "agent." But what do they know about the business? Find out. A reputable agent should have a website with a list of their clients. Start there. What's their background in the publishing biz? How long have they been agenting? There are some watchdog sites – like "Predators and Editors" – that issue warnings about certain names, so use your old pal Google.

3. You need to be businesslike about the relationship. Don't jump at the first bite. Talk to the agent by phone. Ask some questions, see how you click personally. Be objective about

this. From the agent's side it's business; it should be from your side, too.

4. You are probably unrealistic about what an agent can do for you. Having an agent doesn't guarantee a contract. And just because an agent doesn't get you a sale doesn't mean he or she is the problem. It might be your writing, or your timing. A good agent will suggest ways to overcome market weaknesses, but ultimately you have to take charge of improving as a writer. And you'd better do it, because there are a bunch of other writers out there who are.

5. Your agent has many clients; you have only one agent. Don't expect all the attention. Don't expect immediate return of phone calls, unless it's a publishing emergency. Don't expect immediate return of emails unless it is an issue affecting your professional life, like, right now.

6. But agents aren't mind readers, either. If you have a question or issue, contact them. Don't let your frustrations build to the point where it affects your writing.

7. Agents are human beings. "Thank You" notes (real ones, made out of
paper, sent with a stamp) do mean something. So do Starbucks cards and chocolate.

8. Agents are professionals, so approach them as a professional. Don't waste their time. Learn to be concise.

9. Read blogs by agents, but don't let the plethora of information freak you out. Ultimately the most important thing is your writing, the thing you have most control over. Keep coming up with ideas and keep growing as a writer.

10. Fred Allen, the famous radio comedian, once said, "You can take all the sincerity in Hollywood and put it into a

gnat's navel, and still have room for two caraway seeds and an agent's heart." I get to tell that joke because I'm a former lawyer and had to put up with lawyer jokes all the time. But now the truth. The overwhelming majority of agents I've met at conferences love books and authors and want the best for both. So approach agents professionally. They *want* to like you. Show them what you've got. Don't be dull and don't be desperate. It's a tough business out there right now and it's not just writers feeling it, it's agents, too. Everybody in this profession has to keep slugging.

Consider Your Worth: Getting an Agent

1. If you have an agent, are your expectations realistic? Think about it from the agent's point of view. If you had fifty clients to keep happy, would you expect to be able to give any one of them unlimited time and hand holding?

2. If you don't have an agent, consider what you need to do in order to get one: a killer concept comes first. Have you really put it through the wringer? Had other eyes look at it and tell you what you need to know? Do you then know how to put together a professional looking proposal? Are you prepared to go to a writer's conference that offers appointments with agents? Are you ready to act like a professional with them?

3. All the training you need for these matters is available online and in books. Create a self study program, gather materials, and make a two-week "Boot Camp" for yourself on how to care for, or get, an agent.

Energy to Write

We are biological machines, and need energy input lest the

law of entropy reduce us to non-functioning blobs of carbon and water.

This is especially true for writers, who not only have to produce but have to have minds that provide fresh ideas and wonderful characters and sharp dialogue.

So here are some of the things I do to get going.

Like millions of writers before me, I start the day with freshly brewed coffee. I make it at home or sometimes go off to Starbucks with my laptop and imbibe there. There is as much to the comfort factor as there is to the buzz, I think. I just like having something warm to drink as I write.

I've been gratified by all the recent science showing the health benefits of a few cups of coffee. A few. I don't overdo it. I remember that Balzac thought of thick, black coffee as something of a magic drug. The guy was a speed freak without knowing it. He drank up to 50 cups of the stuff a day. And died from it, at age 51.

What would he have done with Red Bull? I shudder to think.

Exercise. I shoot baskets and run around at a local park, talk long walks, treadmill, ride my bike. Keeping the body honed – which is, thankfully, a relative term (you hear me, David Beckham?) – is essential for the right working of the mind.

An added benefit of the workouts is that the "boys in the basement" are busy if I've spent previous hours investing heavily in a project. That's Stephen King's great metaphor for the writer's subconscious. It pays to keep them happy so they don't go on strike.

I'm a morning person, so like to get as much of this done early as I can. I try to do a "furious 500" words as soon as possible. It makes the rest of the writing day go so much better.

At about 1 p.m. I tend to power down for a couple of hours—meaning I'm not at my creative best. Around 1:30 or 2 I usually take a power nap. I can put my feet up on my desk and nod off for 15 – 20 minutes, wake up refreshed.

I've recently tried something that has supercharged these mini-slumbers. Just before I close my eyes, I take a swig of a 5 Hour Energy drink. Not the whole thing. About a third. Then I sleep, and when I wake up I've got this jolt of creative energy that seems to continue without a "crash."

I've learned there is something medically valid to this. It takes 15-20 minutes for caffeine to kick in, so the timing is right for this type of power nap. You get both the benefit of sleep and energy infusion.

I don't do this every day. I don't want to get dependent. But if I need to be working heavy on a project in the afternoon, I'll give it a go.

Sometimes I write standing up, as I'm doing now on my AlphaSmart Neo, on a counter in my house. There's some added energy when you write standing up. I don't know why that is, but I don't need to know, do I?

One last thing. I try to leave off my previous day's writing at a mid-point of some kind, so I'm ready to fly right back into it. Hemingway used to write half a sentence before knocking off. I first read what I wrote yesterday, clean it up, then I'm ready to dive into the day's work.

Consider Your Worth: More Energy

1. Take a good look at your health. Create an objective report, even if you have to bring your doctor in to do it.

2. Can you exercise more? Find a way to do 10% more than you're doing right now. That's a start.

3. How can you modify your eating habits to get more energy? Don't think of overhauling everything, just modify at the moment. Baby steps.

4. Are you getting enough rest at night? Consider varying your patterns to accomplish this. For example, too much alcohol intake before bed disturbs good sleep patterns. You may also need to "quiet down" before going to sleep. Reading is a perfect way to do that.

5. Explore the power nap. It may take you a couple of months to train your body, but it can be done.

a. Start by getting into a quiet place (or putting on soft music and ear phones) and either lie down or put your feet up somehow.

b. Tell yourself you will wake up in twenty minutes. Look at the clock. Then close your eyes and imagine the time twenty minutes hence. Mentally say, "I will wake up at ___."

c. Keep your eyes closed and breath rhythmically. As you do, with each slow breath, count down from 30. See the number as a light on a score board, and each breath ticks off one more number.

d. Don't worry if you don't sleep at first. At the very least, you'll be relaxing for twenty minutes, and that's a positive good in and of itself.

Do Not Go Gentle Onto That Good Page

Do not go gentle into that good night . . .Rage, rage against the dying of the light. – Dylan Thomas

Brett Favre, one of the best quarterbacks ever to play the game of football, was supposed to be over-the-hill at 40. But in 2009 he finished what is probably his finest season and almost got the Minnesota Vikings to the Super Bowl. In the NFC championship game against the New Orleans Saints, he took a beating. He was on the turf constantly, sometimes under 380 pounds of beef. In the second half he got his left ankle twisted, limped off, got re-taped, and came back into the game. But for a number of turnovers by his teammates and one ill-timed interception, the Vikes would have won. It was an inspiring performance, adding to his legend.

Robert B. Parker, creator of Spenser and one of the most prolific authors of our time, died January 18, 2009, at the age of 77. He was supposed to be over-the-hill, too. Some critics thought he was, but most readers did not. Parker was turning out books to the very end, and not just in his Spenser series. He had other series going, including Jesse Stone, which Tom Selleck has brought to TV. He also wrote stand alones and Westerns.

He was reportedly about 40 pages into a new Spenser novel when he died at his desk of a heart attack.

For a writer, baby, that's the way to go. I only hope I've just typed the last page.

Regardless, Favre and Parker are two guys who refused to go gentle into that good night. To write well, there has to be a part of you that is determined to rage, rage against the dying of the light--and against rejection, criticism and the slough of despond.

A knock on Parker in the latter phase of his career was that he wrote too much, sacrificing quality. Well, that's between him and his readers. He wrote, they bought, they enjoyed, maybe some got frustrated. But the relationship was lasting, and the man was doing what he loved.

If you love to write, you'll find a way to do it. No one can promise how that'll turn out. No one can guarantee you a publishing contract. But you'll never get close if you don't rage a little, and turn that into determination to keep writing, keep going, keep producing the words.

My grandfather and my mom both wanted to be writers. So they wrote. My grandfather wrote historical fiction and ended up self-publishing some of it. It's really not bad at all, but it's very niche stuff. Yet I remember him being proud of it, and it pleased the family.

My mom wrote radio scripts while she was in college in WWII. I have a whole bunch of them. Quite good. She worked on a small local newspaper when I was a kid. I remember, when I was twelve or so, finding a short story she wrote, a sci-fi kind of thing, that had a cool twist ending. She never got it published but it influenced at least one young writer--me.

So do not go gentle onto that good page. At the very least you'll know you're alive, and you won't walk around (as Murray says in *A Thousand Clowns*) with that wide-eyed look some people put on their faces so no one will know their head's asleep.

Rage a little, throw the heat, write.

Consider Your Worth: What Fires You Up?

1. Make a list of all the things in this world that make you mad. Write it fast. Keep going.

2. Make a list of all the things that make you feel alive, things you love.

3. Refer to these lists when you are considering your next story. How can you get one or more of these items in the tale?

Blown Calls

Maybe you read about the terrible blown call in the 2010 baseball season. Pitcher Armando Galarraga of the Detroit Tigers was on the verge of doing what only twenty other pitchers in Major League history have accomplished: pitch a perfect game (a no-hitter wherein no opposing player even reaches first base).

It was two outs in the 9th inning. Only one player left to go. But then the Cleveland Indians' Jason Donald hit a grounder to the first base side. Galarraga ran over to cover. He caught the throw and stepped on the bag a split second before Donald's foot.

In other words, Donald was out. Only he wasn't.

He wasn't because a veteran umpire, Jim Joyce, blew the call. He was in position to call it correctly, and did not. Because there is no instant replay review in MLB, the call stands. No perfect game. Not even a no-hitter.

To their everlasting credit, all parties concerned handled things with class. Umpire Joyce manned up and owned it.

He wept at his mistake. The Detroit fans showed class, too, by giving the highly regarded Joyce a standing ovation when he came out to umpire the next game. And Galarraga and the Tigers did not do what 90% of other players and teams would. They did not overturn water coolers or cry and moan and complain.

Nor should they have. This is the reality of baseball. Human error by umpires is *part of the game.* You accept that going in. You know it's going to happen. You want to change the rules and bring in replay, fine. But as it stands, blown calls are as much a part of baseball as peanuts and beer.

It's like the publishing business, and life. Bad stuff happens to good people, and good manuscripts.

You get turned down by an agent in summary fashion. Your submission gets kicked at a publishing house for some reason other than the writing itself. You see someone else – maybe even a friend – score a great contract or get on the bestseller list. And it hacks you off, because you know you can write just as well, or better.

Life hands you blown calls. So what do you do about it?

When my son was first pitching Little League, he had a tendency to let a bad play or a home run upset him. So early on I made this rule with him. "You are allowed one *'Dang it!'* And you can hit your glove as hard as you want. But that's it. Then you go back to pitching to the next guy."

That's what he learned to do, and in fact won a championship game that way.

So you get that rejection, or see that unfairness. You can have one *"Dang it!"* (or its adult equivalent). I'll let you feel it for fifteen minutes. But that's it. Don't hang onto it. Don't go moaning all over the Internet. Don't yell at your spouse or kick your dog.

Instead, turn that energy into action – *by writing.*

Here's what I love about being a writer. Every day is new. Every day I get to wake up and pound those keys and keep going. It doesn't matter to me if I get a setback, a bad review, a rejection. I can keep punching, and I will keep punching until groundhog delivers my mail.

Writing on the Move

Been doing a lot of speaking this year, which involves one of my least favorite things: Checking into airports. I love the speaking once I arrive. It's the getting there I'm not always thrilled with.

But if I can redeem the time by writing, I figure I break even on the travel. So here are some of the things I do to get the most out of my travel time.

First, I pre-plan. I do much better if I have one or two definite goals for the flight. So the day before my trip I decide what part of my WIP I'll work on. I spend some time preparing the scenes I'm going to write, figuring out what I want to accomplish.

Then I set a word quota so I have an objective firmly in mind. This provides a reachable goal to work toward.

I carry a file folder with printed notes I deem of use. This is for those times when they don't let you have any electronics going on the plane.

I get the airport early so I have plenty of time to make it through security. At the gate area I scope out a place to sit and work, usually at some inactive gate nearby. Fewer people. If it's an hour or more before boarding, I grab a coffee and take out the laptop and go. If it's half an hour or less, I usually work on the written notes.

Onboard, I generally have a window seat. That way I can get seated and get working without having to worry about people getting up during the flight.

In the air I put on my Bose noise cancelling headphones and get the iTunes going. I write to movie soundtracks, which I've divided into lists depending on the mood of the scene. Usually I'm writing suspense, so I've got my Hitchcock scores and others at the ready.

And so it goes. When ordered to power down, I still have my written notes, or a paperback. Yes, I still carry paperbacks on planes. So sue me.

That's my flyboy routine. On the ground, when I have to go someplace where I know I'll have to wait, I might take my AlphaSmart with me. Again, I have pre-planned what I want to write, so I'm not twiddling my fingers over the keyboard.

Here's the deal. We all have a finite time on this orb, and I want to get in as much writing as I can. Redeeming the time this way keeps me optimistic and productive.

Do I ever take a vacation from writing? Of course. My wife will tell you. We go away to lovely spot for some R & R. Conversations usually start like this: "Jim? Jim! There's a great sunset over here. Jim, what are you thinking about?"

"Hm? What? Sorry, right."

"Um, you have to look out the window to see it."

"See what?"

"The sunset."

"Right, right."

"So, are you going to come to the window?"

"Just a sec, just a sec . . ."

Consider Your Worth: Redeeming Time

1. Assess your daily schedule. Block out those times that are taken up, and those times that are free.

2. Make a writing schedule that allows you to write a quota of words.

3. Keep track of times you can "snatch" for writing. Can you detect a pattern?

The Home Stretch

So I'm entering the last month on my WIP. First drafting, deadline wire up ahead. I find this horserace to be a time of great exhilaration, desperation, excitement, consternation and frequent trips to Starbucks.

Even though I've done this dozens of times, it never feels like, "Hey, I've got this so nailed. No problem!"

I'm looking at all the story threads, balls in the air, knowing the ending I'm heading for but wondering how

I'll get there. In my head, I know I will, because I always do, somehow.

But in the heat of battle, writing each day, I feel like a Spartan trying to hold off Xerxes at Thermopylae. And I suppose I wouldn't have it any other way (especially if I was ripped like Gerard Butler).

Here's why I wouldn't. To be in this battle is to be alive. As Jack London once said, "I'd rather be ashes than dust! I would rather that my spark should burn out in a brilliant blaze than it should be stifled by dry-rot. I would rather be a superb meteor, every atom of me in magnificent glow, than a sleepy and permanent planet. The function of man is to live, not to exist."

Writing well is about being alive, about being out on the wire over Niagara Falls, about jumping on the back of Bucephalus and grabbing some mane. Ray Bradbury once described his writing day as getting up each morning and exploding, then spending the rest of the day putting the pieces together.

It's about running a race ahead of a mob of angry, torch bearing townsfolk. It's about skiing down a mountain ahead of an avalanche.

It's about being open to all the fantastic things you can't control, then finding ways to form a pleasing shape out of them.

Being alive, truly alive, means a degree of uncertainty. It means risk. If there's no risk, there's not going to be any lasting reward. If your reach does not exceed your grasp, you'll just keep grabbing the same old leaves.

This is nowhere more pronounced than when I'm heading home on a novel. Now is that time. I'm shouting like Slim

Pickens riding the atomic bomb at the end of *Dr. Strangelove.*
When I am at the keys and moving the fingers, I am kicking all doubts into the pit. "This is Sparta!"

Who is a Real Writer?

A writer who is a real writer is a rebel who never stops. --
William Saroyan

A writer is someone for whom writing is more difficult than it is for other people. --**Thomas Mann**

So who is a "real" writer? Who can legitimately say, without fear of embarrassment, "I'm a writer" when asked the question of vocation?

Is it someone who has decided this morning to become a writer? And then goes to Starbucks and writes *Chapter One* and begins?

Or do you have some dues to pay?

Speaking of pay, to you have to get some to be a real writer?

There was a guy who used to hang out at my local Starbucks, typing poems on an honest to goodness typewriter. He said that was the best way for him. He was about 30, and had the hipster look down. He'd type a poem for someone in exchange for whatever they wanted to pay.

He was, I guess, a "professional writer." He got paid, didn't he?

Should we simply distinguish between those who make a living, or a substantial amount of their living, writing, from those who want to be able to do that?

Or is the little old retired lady who has written the humor corner for her church newspaper for twenty years, getting no pay, but being enjoyed by a readership of fifty, a real writer?

Or does any of this matter?

Personally, I found it difficult to tell people I was a writer before I was published. I knew I was, I was committed to it. But it felt funny. When I got my first contract, it was still hard to say. When I got my first multiple book contract, it got easier. Because I'd worked really hard at it and finally it was paying off.

But with self-publishing via e-books getting to be so easy, people can be "multi-published" with a click of the "Upload" button. Writers all?

A novelist friend of mine told me this:

I remember being in the library years ago, back when I was struggling with whether or not I could legitimately say I was a writer. I think it was even before I'd completed the 40,000-word fantasy "novel" that I have let no one see (and which no longer exists, I don't think).

In the stacks I stumbled upon a nonfiction book on writing fiction. Don't have a clue what it was. But I thumbed through it and found a section that addresses this question, and the answer it gave was enormously freeing to me.

It said something to the effect that if you constantly have

65

story ideas and/or or characters coming to your mind, thrilling your soul and firing your energies, making you want to sit down and write them, you are a writer. Even if you never get published. Even if you never complete a novel.

Shortly after that, I began writing in earnest. With permission, almost. And not too long after that, I got published.

Another friend said this:

To call yourself a writer, you have to engage in it daily with some exchange of money between you and a publisher. Or a client. Or a film or TV company. It has to in some ways be your vocation. As to whether or not you're making a living wage isn't so much the catalyst, but that you are pursuing jobs and publishing your work FOR MONEY. Otherwise, it's a hobby, a fascination, a desire, a work in progress.

A third friend, who has made a living as a freelance writer for many years, told me:

To me, to truly be a writer, you have to pass a gantlet of editors, critics, peers, and the marketplace. I never thought of it as a distinction between writers and *professional* writers. To me it was a distinction between writers and the rest of the world. Not everyone who types up manuscripts and submits them to publishers is a writer. In my mind, until you have earned the right to call yourself a writer, don't call yourself a writer. So, while I don't blame anyone for saying, "Anyone can be a writer" or "All you have to do is write," these statements really sadden me. I realize that what for me is a holy calling and an ennobled profession has in many ways lost that distinction forever. If anyone with a

keyboard and enough money to upload a file to Xulon Press or iUniverse can call himself a "writer," then everything I set my sights on from the time I was nine years old has become relatively meaningless.

Maybe my view is best summed up by the two quotes at the top of this post. If you're a real writer, it's going to be difficult, because you can't just throw anything out there. You have to sweat and bleed to learn to write. And if you want to be a writer, you just can't give up. You do have to have a little bit of the rebel in you, because people will probably think you're a bit nutty (while secretly envying your passion).

Consider Your Worth: Being a Real Writer

1. Do you have an inner drive to write that won't stop, even when you're the most frustrated?

2. Do you spend more time writing than you do thinking about writing?

3. What do you want your obituary to say? Seriously. Write it. Does it have something about your writing in it?

Growing as a Writer

If you're going to be a writer, I mean really taking this writing thing seriously, you've got to continue to grow. Purposely. Planned out. Find ways to get better. Read books (not just for pleasure, but to see what other writers do), comb through writing books and *Writer's Digest,* try stuff, take risks. The alternative is to stagnate, and who wants that? In any endeavor?

I thought about this recently as I watched some of John Wayne's early movies via inexpensive (translation: cheapie) DVDs. John Wayne was not John Wayne when he started out. (Actually, his real name was Marion Morrison. How long would he have lasted with that moniker?)

After working as an extra for a couple of years, this former USC football player was, at age 22, plucked from obscurity by director Raoul Walsh for a big budget Western, *The Big Trail* (1930). The movie flopped, and Wayne spent the next nine years making low budget westerns for studios on what was called "Poverty Row" in Hollywood.

The poorest of these studios was an outfit called Lone Star. Here is where we see John Wayne trying to find himself as an actor. It was a hard search, especially when he was stuck in such poorly written, clunkily acted, one hour oaters. Pictures like *Riders of Destiny* (1933), where he was billed as Singin' Sandy. (That's right. John Wayne as a singing cowboy! Only his singing was dubbed – badly – as Wayne pretended to play the guitar – badly.)

Wayne's acting here was wooden and uncertain. The only direction he seemed to get was to smile a lot, and that got a tad creepy. This was one forgettable actor.

But by 1936 he had moved one notch up, to Republic Pictures. In *Winds of the Wasteland*, for example, he seems like a different actor. Here is the real John Wayne. His acting is understated and sure. He's even started walking that famous walk.

What happened? Wayne made a decision to grow, to get better. A lot of credit for that apparently goes to the legendary stuntman, Yakima Canutt, a real "man's man" back in the day when that was an okay thing to be. Wayne copied Canutt's low, confident way of speaking, and his walk. And he stopped smiling all the time. Wayne was also befriended by an old character actor named Paul Fix, who gave Wayne acting tips, including the admonition not to furrow that famous brow so much.

The results were promising. Wayne learned. He grew.

Still, Wayne would probably have remained a B actor all his life (maybe he would have had a TV show like Hopalong Cassidy in the 1950s) had it not been for his friendship with John Ford. When the famous director wanted to make a Western in 1939 called *Stagecoach*, he got resistance (Westerns weren't in vogue). When he insisted that Wayne play the Ringo Kid, he got turned down flat. But Ford wouldn't budge, and eventually put a deal together with an indie producer. His going to bat for Wayne was what made him a star.

But Wayne didn't stop there. Though he never would be mistaken for Brando or Olivier, he did reach down for extra in movies like *Red River* (1948), *She Wore a Yellow Ribbon* (1949), *Sands of Iwo Jima* (1949, Academy Award nomination), *The Searchers* (1956), *True Grit* (1969, Academy Award for Best Actor) and *The Shootist* (1976), his very last film.

And of course, John Wayne became an icon, *still* ranking as a favorite movie star worldwide.

So, if you want to make a mark as a writer, you grow. Consciously. That doesn't bring any guarantees. John Wayne himself needed a couple of lucky breaks to get the heights he enjoyed. But he made himself ready, as you should.

Consider Your Worth: Make a Plan

1. Make a plan.

2. Start taking action on that plan.

3. Take some form of action every day on your plan.

4. Revisit and renew (or revise) the plan once a year.

When Should You Quit Writing?

At a writers conference recently, one of the attendees (who has been coming for years and still hasn't broken into publication) sat down with me and said, "I want you to tell me, straight up, if I'm just spinning my wheels here. I've been trying so long and never get anywhere. I want to know if I should just quit and forget the whole thing."

That's a good question and deserves an expanded answer. So . . . here's mine.

First, I know many immediately jump to the thought, "If you have to ask, then quit. Real writers never quit!" That's a little too flip. This can be an incredibly frustrating business at every level, from query rejection to book returns, from agent hunting to bad reviews. So genuine feelings of angst are real and I don't want to downplay them.

Still, there is a kernel of truth in the statement. To write well, you have to have an inner desire that can't be doused by setbacks. Yes, the flame may dim when you're hit hard, but in a real writer it keeps coming back, like one of those trick candles you put on a birthday cake.

You have to be like Rudy, from the movie of the same name. He knew his chances of ever getting into a real game were virtually nil. And every day at practice he'd get his head knocked off by the varsity players getting ready for the week's game.

Bam. Bam. Bam. That's what this writing thing feels like sometimes. But you get up and keep hitting back.

You have to know, going in, that you need to develop Rhino skin to survive. The good news is you *can* develop it. Every time you come back from a set-back and *write some more,* you create a little more of that protective coating, that inner strength.

So if you can look at the big picture, with all the odds stacked against you . . .if you can understand full well that you will be taking hit after hit . . .if you can understand all that and still have that inner ferret that says, "Write, dang you!" – then no, you should not quit.

Okay, I know some of you are saying, "That's the same old rah-rah stuff I hear at every writer's conference. Easy for *him* to say . . ."

Well, ladies and germs, we don't get very far without the rah-rah stuff. It's the stuff of Churchill on the BBC during the Blitz, or Henry V at Agincourt, or dare I say Aragorn at the big black gate: "This day we fight!"

So hear these words resounding in your head: It's always too soon to quit.

Yes, rejection hurts. So, let it. Let it hurt for about fifteen minutes. Then go to your keyboard and write, "I resolve . . ." and continue writing for fifteen minutes.

And, as long as you're not quitting, you can do things like this:

1. Get ideas.

2. Play the first line game (come up with a bunch of first lines, choose the best one, and write)

3. Write a short story.

4. Write your memoirs (hey, you've got a family, right?)

5. Write an essay.

6. Write blog post or a meaty comment for a blog.

7. Study the craft. Read a writing book with a highlighter in hand.

8. Finish that project you've been putting off.

9. Eat one cheeseburger, with everything on it, once a month.

10. Keep writing.

Remember, every moment you spend writing is a moment spent not fretting about your writing (h/t Dennis Palumbo).

So don't quit.

The Writing Craft

A Glimpse At My Writing Notebook

When I first set out to learn the craft of writing fiction, I went after it the way Jack London said you should go after inspiration: with a club. I read and studied and practiced and found out what worked. I formulated techniques for myself, experimenting like some mad Edison, until I hit on something that was effective.

And all the while I took copious notes. I was writing screenplays and novels, and keeping a record of my processes. This I would revise from time to time, to reflect new things I'd learned.

Eventually I had a big old notebook I called my Master Novel Writing Process. And I did what I used to do in law school. I had a huge outline here, and then I condensed it down into a shorter outline for easy reference.

I thought you might be interested in seeing this shorter outline. It might give you some ideas about how to approach your own novel. Feel free to use what you find of interest. Note, some of the verbiage may have come from other resources that I've now forgotten. These were, after all, my personal working notes. So if I've inadvertently quoted another author, my apologies. In my other writing books I always acknowledge sources.

Ready? Have a look:

1. NURTURE AN IDEA

• Think BACK COVER COPY. Start brainstorming, alternating between cover copy and creative, stream of consciousness letter/conversation to yourself, flowing, asking questions: FIRST and FOREMOST, why do I want to tell this story? Who might the characters be? What's going on? What do you find interesting about this or that? Force answers to go deeper. Ask WHY? WHAT IF? a lot.

• Annotate the above, and do again. Repeat.

2. LAUNCHING PAD

• A lead and his situation
• What he will want badly
• Who opposes him
• Potential climactic scene, disaster. [Imagine this over and over as a movie scene. How does it play? How can you make it twisty or unanticipated?]
• Possible THEME: Simple sentence of the big idea. "Justice prevails over corruption." (This may change after first draft)

3. FRESHNESS TEST

- What UNIQUE TWIST or angle can you give this idea?
- What's unique about the CHARACTER?
- What's unique about the SETTING?
- What's unique about the RELATIONSHIPS?
- What's unique about the PLOT?
- Turn all clichés ON THEIR HEAD
- What is the "Oh wow!" quotient?
- Where is the passionate heart of this story for YOU and the Lead?
- IMPORTANT: Do you have EMOTIONAL FERVOR for the story?

4. PRELIMINARY RESEARCH

- Necessary?
- Quick answers. Do the "fill in" research AFTER first draft.

5. PLOTTING

- Brainstorm a list of **POSSIBLE MAJOR** rising action events in the story.
- For mystery, brainstorm the crime, with all sorts of twists and turns, and then work backward. Or the courtroom drama at the end, etc.
- Subplot? Personal? Carries what theme? How does it connect? Life lesson here?
- **Outline a Climactic Scene.** "Know where you're going." [Do it as a movie scene in your mind! Make it fresh. Is it telling YOU the plot?]
- Supreme Test of conflict of desires?
- Sacrifice?
- Ticking clock?
- TWISTS: 1 "raise stakes"; 1 "secret revealed"; 1 MAJOR setback (just before climax is good). Brainstorm!!
- Work it, revise it, for a week. Look for connections of

past with other characters. Do it in a week. See if you want to go on. CONNECT PLOT AND CHARACTERS.
STAKES

• What will be lost to the lead if he doesn't get his goal?
• Why should we care about the lead? Is there high human worth through:
• high principles and code of person conduct? How will that code be tested at the end? IOW, how will the hero have to sacrifice something (personal health, psychological health, etc.) to remain true?
• Do you have honesty, integrity, loyalty, kindness, bravery, respect, trust and love of others? Choose wisely.
• Passion. How is the lead passionate, and why?
• Who does the lead care about besides herself?
• Choose: a torturous need, a consuming fear, an aching regret, a visible dream, a passionate longing, an inescapable ambition, an inner lack, a fatal weakness, a noble ideal, an unavoidable obligation

GET FEEDBACK ON STORY FROM MY LOVELY WIFE AND OTHERS.

6. CHARACTER CREATION

LEAD AND MAIN OPPOSITION: (Do quick character journal on the following for each):
• Sex & Age.
• Dominant impression (x2?)
• Vulnerability - in what way is the character vulnerable?
• What is character's greatest FEAR?
• A shaping experience from the past. A secret wound?
• TAGS of speech, mannerisms.
• How is the character STRONG? Show COURAGE? Q Factor? Characters may start out scared, but GROW STRONGER AS STORY PROCEEDS!
• A DEEP NEED, the void that the character needs to

overcome to reclaim self-worth/happiness. This comes as a result of a DEFEAT (WOUND) suffered in the past. It should RELATE to the main plot. IOW, what the character does will in some way overcome this. The PAST defeat, part of the backstory, COMES BACK INTO the present story in some form, through the characters involved, etc.

• How is your lead "round"? How can she surprise us in a convincing way? (Forster) How is she individualized? What is the most spontaneous, witty, or outrageous thing the character might do? Why not put that scene in the novel?

• What will be the LIFE LESSON LEARNED/INNER CHANGE?

• An IMMEDIATE want. This is the initial problem, change, need that the character is facing in the opening chapter. Also, HINT AT the DEEP WANT here. It should show the lead in her STORY WORLD, the "normal world" (i.e., profession)

• A STORY WANT, the main want that will be the objective of the story, with the confrontations, etc.

• How will the lead show FORGIVENESS and/or SELF SACRIFICE?

• Choose a TEMPERAMENT.

• Choose a FLAW or FOIBLE.

• CAST the character. Get a magazine picture, start 1 page dossier.

• Do a "voice journal" of character talking on all manner of things.

• Why do I love this character? What about him "turns me on"?

• Do TIMELINE of life (on back of 1 page dossier).

• "Writing up long life histories of each character is nonsense." (Scott Meredith)

7. SUBPLOTS

• Must connect with and enrich the main plot. Connect

them early, or show how they are going to converge.
• Romantic subplot, theme subplot, or both?
• List characters, and look for "nodes of conjunction."
What deep, multiple connections are possible? Interweave
character relationships.

8. OPENING SCENE

• How does it HOOK THEM FROM THE START?
• How does the opening conflict "bridge"? Inciting
incident? Interruption?
• Hint at THEME. (Can go back and do later)
• Portend trouble. Make it EMOTIONAL for the
character! Aim for the HEART!
• Use character in action to establish **setting** and tone.

9. WRITING SCENES

• What FEELING do you want from this scene?
• What SETTING helps the mood?
• What is the character's PURPOSE in the scene?
• What is the CONFLICT here? Every scene!
• What is the EMOTION in the character?
• Is this a SCENE or SEQUEL? Do the three parts.
• Is this scene primarily PLOT or CHARACTER
DEEPENING?
• Be sure to think of the character's EMOTIONAL
REACTIONS. Use SENSORY DETAILS + CHARACTER
REACTION.
• Visualize the scene and set down a few key words
beforehand. **MIND MAP SCENE, LOOKING FOR
FRESHNESS AND SURPRISES.**

10. STEP BACK AND LAYER

• After about 20,000 words or so, stop and step back
and see what you have.

• After 50,000 words, deepen the characters and motivations, and go back and "layer" them into the first draft. Gives added dimension and directions.

Character Arc?

I always enjoy listening to Lee Child. He's got this great English accent and droll delivery, and says things that are usually contrarian and funny.

At last year's conference, Child was on a panel when the subject of character change came up. A constant drum beat in fiction classes and books on writing is that your character must change in some way. There must be a "character arc."

"Why?" Child asked rhetorically. "There doesn't have to be character change. We don't need no stinkin' arcs."

Everybody in the room cracked up. Child went on to explain that he loves Dom Perignon champagne, and he wants it to taste the same each time. And so, too, he wants his Jack Reacher books to offer the same pleasurable experience every time out. Reacher doesn't change. Reacher does his thing. It's how he does it that provides the pleasure.

And I do love a good Reacher.

Then another of my favorite authors spoke. Michael Connelly was interviewed in a packed convention. The Harry Bosch books are the best series maybe . . . ever. Connelly spoke about his decision twenty years ago to have Bosch age chronologically. So in each book Bosch is about a year older.

And that means he changes. He has varying degrees of inner development. Talk about your arcs! It's still going on and it's a wonder to behold.

So there you have it, a tale of two writers and two approaches, both of which work. They provide different experiences and readers can choose which they like best — or go with both, for variety.

When I teach about character work, I do say that a Lead character does not have to change in a fundamental way. For example, in the film *The Fugitive,* Dr. Richard Kimble does not become a new man. He does not have to discover his "true self." What he has to do is *grow stronger* as he meets extraordinary challenges.

Similarly, Marge Gunderson in *Fargo* does not change, but shows her inner strength by solving a horrific crime, far beyond what she's had to deal with before.

So in this kind of thriller, the character is already who he or she needs to be, but gets tested and strengthened.

A nice wrinkle to this type of story is when the Lead's strength inspires another character to change. That's what happens in *The Fugitive.* Kimble's relentless search for the killer of his wife turns Sam Gerard from a lawman who "doesn't care" about the facts of a case, to caring very much indeed.

In *Casablanca,* you have both kinds of change. Not only does Rick Blaine change radically, from a man who wants to be left alone to one who joins the war effort, but so does the little French captain, Louis. Rick's act of self sacrifice at the end inspires Louis to leave Casablanca with Rick, also fight the Nazis. It is, of course, the beginning of a beautiful friendship.

One of the most important questions you can ask at the beginning of your novel is whether the main character will undergo fundamental change, or just get stronger. It needs to be one or the other.

Ten Ideas From One Article

When I teach, one of my themes is that the writer has to become a walking idea factory. You have to come up with raw story material all the time, nurture the nuggets, and figure out a way to turn some of them into novels or stories. And it has to be ongoing, week after week.

Why? Because it guarantees you won't be stuck looking for material. You'll always have a bag of unrefined gold to dip into. It also exercises your imagination, builds it up, which will serve you in the writing itself. They call the people who work on Disney theme parks "Imagineers". That has to be you, too.

I teach a lot of ways to get and nurture ideas (see chapter 3 of *Plot & Structure*), but here's an example of one, called Bleeding an Article Dry. I set a goal to come up with ten ideas from a single news item. I'm going to show you how that might look in a moment. But first, you need to remember a couple of things:

1. Do not censor yourself. In brainstorming, there are no "wrong" answers.

2. You get good ideas by coming up with lots of ideas, then selecting the ones that are most promising. Don't expect each one to be a gem.

3. Go relatively quickly. By the time you're at number five

or so, your writer's brain will be kicking into gear and getting stuff from your gray matter you didn't know was there.

4. Go with tangents. You're not tied to the facts of the story. For example, my first idea below suggested something totally bizarre. I jotted it down as 1a.

Okay, here goes. The story picked at random is this item, from ABC news online:

Paradise Lost: Lawful Beach Upgrade or State Land Grab? Supreme Court Hears Arguments in Florida Property Rights Case

Nestled along the pristine white beaches of the Florida Panhandle town of Destin, is the home of Nancy and Slade Lindsay, who say when they bought their property 12 years ago they fulfilled a lifelong dream to own a private beach.

But now the Lindsays say the state of Florida has dashed that dream by illegally taking their beach front property and allowing the public to use it without any proper compensation.

"They are literally taking our property," Lindsay says. "Changing our deeds, changing our property boundaries, no compensation and no tax breaks."

The controversy arose when Walton County officials-- citing dangerous beach erosion-- stepped in to renourish beaches along a 6.9 mile stretch using taxpayer money. Florida's Beach and Shore Preservation Act authorizes publicly funded beach restoration projects to protect critically eroded beaches.

The multimillion dollar project added new sand, reshaped dunes and in some areas substantially increased the size of the beach. But the improvements, according to Florida law, also made that "new" strip of beach behind the Lindsay's home, public property.

The Lindsay's and four other residents along the sandy stretch filed a lawsuit to challenge Florida's actions, yet in the end the state's highest court ruled in favor of Florida.

The homeowners then decided to take their case to the U.S. Supreme Court, arguing that the Florida Supreme Court decision had unconstitutionally deprived them of their property. In legalese the homeowners say that the state court decision constituted a "judicial taking" of their property, which is prohibited by the U.S. Constitution.

Today, the Supreme Court will hear arguments in the case. . .

###

1. What if they bought this property to cover up murders? What if bodies are buried there, dozens of them?

1a) Possible zombie idea here. What if zombies want a beach resort of their own?

2. Legal thriller: someone in the county office has forged their papers. Why?

3. What if the beach is used as a landing point for drug runners? What if they take this beach couple hostage?

4. Maybe some super wealthy developer is causing the erosion somehow, or polluting the beach on purpose. Maybe he wants to cause the taking then swoop in and buy the land from the county as a "savior."

5. What if these rich couples have banded together, but on of the couples is a notorious crime duo with false identities?

James Scott Bell

6. What if the lawyer who takes their case is a double agent paid off by the county?

7. What if one of the Supreme Court justices is a secret partner in a dummy corporation that has plans to develop the land?

The story continues:

. . . Brad Pickle, President of Sea Haven Consulting, who oversaw the beach renourishment program for the County, says Florida was well within its right to improve the beaches.

He says the state did not take away the homeowner's property, it merely created more property between the homeowners land and the ocean. "What you are doing is putting sand in state waters so it is state property to begin with and state property when the project is over with," Pickel said.

But the land owners accuse the state of disguising its desire to open the beaches to more tourists by citing land erosion.

8. What if the landowners take a consultant or the politicians hostage and declare they are like the early Americans holding off the gummint?

9. What if the National Guard has to be brought in?

10. I also look at accompanying photographs, and launch from there. One showed a man looking out at the water on top of weathered beach stairs. What if that guy was suddenly pushed down those rickety stairs? Was it an accident? Or murder?

So I have ten ideas. I may not stop there if I'm cooking. But eventually I'll cease and let the ideas cool off a bit. The next day I'll go through them and maybe add a few I've thought of overnight.

Then I'll think about the most promising (for me) and maybe develop them a little further. Let's say I like number 9. I'll start thinking about what circumstances would lead to the National Guard coming in. I may even do some quick research, as that often leads to more ideas.

Consider Your Worth: Do a 10 for 10

1. Quick. Select a story from the news and spend ten minutes (no more) writing down ten ideas. Go.

2. Select the best three ideas. Think about them for awhile.

3. Select the one idea that seems to hold the most promise. Spend half an hour just brainstorming: write without stopping, jotting whatever comes to your mind. Set this aside for the day.

4. Go back to the document a day later and edit it. Highlight what seems fresh and most interesting to you. The write for another half hour on this. Set aside for another day. Edit the next day.

5. Repeat the process for the other two ideas you came up with.

Serendipity

I started blogging for The Kill Zone on July 26. It's a special date for me, because it also happens to be one that changed my life forever — for it was on a July 26 that I met my wife.

I was at a birthday party for a friend. It had spilled out into the courtyard of his apartment building, where I sat at a table with a couple guys, yakking. I happened to look up and saw a blond vision of loveliness heading up the stairs to the apartment. I turned to my comrades and said, "I'll see you later."

I got to the apartment just as she was hugging my friend. Her back was to me. I silently motioned for my friend to introduce me. And that, as they say, was that. I fell like five tons of brick and mortar. It took me all of two-and-a-half weeks to ask her to marry me. (Perhaps this explains why I favor first page action in my books). Eight months later we were wed and my life has been richly blessed ever since (in no small part due to Cindy's sharp editorial eye; she's always my first reader).

When I think of these events, the word *serendipity* comes to mind. It's a word derived from a Persian fairy tale, *The Three Princes of Serendip* (an ancient name for Sri Lanka). The story tells of an eminent trio making happy discoveries in their travels, through accident and observation. The English writer Horace Walpole coined the term *serendipity* to describe this combination of chance and mental discernment.

Which is a long way of saying that some of the best things that happen to us in life are "happy accidents" because we've shown up, and are aware.

Much of the best writing we do is serendipitous, too. As Lawrence Block, the dean of American crime fiction, put it, "You look for something, find something else, and realize that what you've found is more suited to your needs than what you thought you were looking for."

Doesn't that describe some of the best moments in your writing? I once had a wife character who was supposed to move away for a time, to get out of danger. That's what I'd outlined. But in the heat of a dialogue scene with her husband, she flat out refused to go. Turns out she was right and I was wrong, and the story was better for it.

The way of serendipity is open to every writer, be you an outliner or a seat-of-the-pants type, or anything in between. It's just a matter of showing up and being aware. And the more you write, the more you'll recognize serendipitous moments when they arise.

Consider Your Worth: Ramp Up Your Serendipity

1. Don't just be about imposing your plans on the story to the detriment of happy surprises. Be ready to shift and move.

2. Write what you fear. Go where the risks are in the story. Challenge yourself.

3. Research. When you delve deeply into the areas you're writing about – by reading, talking to experts, or doing something in the field – you inevitably come up with gems that will enliven your story or even change it into something other than what you had planned. And that's not a bad thing.

4. Write first, analyze later. It is in the heat of production that diamonds are formed – a striking image, a line of dialogue, a new character. But you have to be prepared to go with the flow, to play it out and see where things lead.

What's in a Name?

Mystery writers everywhere honor the name of that master detective, Sherrinford Holmes, and his good friend, Ormond Sacker.

Or not.
And what about that great heroine of the Civil War South,
Pansy O'Hara? Remember her?

Of course you don't. Because Margaret Mitchell thankfully
scotched it after briefly considering it for her lead in *Gone
With the Wind*. Props also to Sir Arthur Conan Doyle for
choosing Sherlock Holmes and Dr. John Watson, after
toying those other names.

The name of a Lead character, especially one who will be
the star of a series, is not to be randomly selected. Sherlock
Holmes is perfect. (Doyle admired Oliver Wendell
Holmes, Jr.; Sherlock may have been the name of his
favorite cricket batsman). And Scarlett is just right for
Miss O'Hara.

Travis McGee, the popular creation of John D. MacDonald,
has a sound like the character himself--living on a
houseboat, few cares in the world, tough when he needs to
be.

Could any gumshoe be tougher than Sam Spade?

Ignatius J. Reilly and Myrna Minkoff definitely belong in
John Kennedy Toole's oddly structured comic novel, *A
Confederacy of Dunces*.

Here is what went into naming my own series character,
Ty Buchanan, whose latest appearance is in *Try Fear*.

Tyler is from *Fight Club*. Tyler Durden (played by Brad Pitt
in the film) is primal, nihilistic, violent. In *Try Dying*, the
first book in my series, Ty Buchanan has to contend with
similar feelings as his world is turned upside down. An
up-and-coming lawyer in LA, Ty has it all. But his fiancé is

killed (on page 1) and when he goes looking for answers, he's forced into a street existence that both engenders and requires a hard-edged response.

Buchanan is from a favorite Western of mine, *Buchanan Rides Alone* (1958, dir. Budd Boetticher), starring the iconic Randolph Scott. He is, in the best western tradition, an anti-hero and loner, but with a strong inner code of honor. He doesn't look for trouble, but when it finds him, he fights. And he always displays an insouciant good humor.

I wanted these two dynamics to play out within Ty Buchanan. They provide counterpoint and inner conflict, as the Buchanan side is often at odds with the Durden aspect. Thus, the name.

So put some real thought into the naming of your Lead characters. The better it sounds, and the more consonant with your purposes, the better it serve you and your readers.

Shake, Rattle and Write

On August 16, 1977, Elvis left the building for good.

He was found face down in his bathroom at Graceland. The official cause of death was heart failure. He was forty-two years old.

Elvis immediately took up residence in the pantheon of pop culture icons. The Soviet newspaper *Pravda* announced that America could be thanked for three things: Mickey Mouse, Coca-Cola and Elvis Presley. A new industry – Elvis imitation – sprang up, bringing employment to thousands. In fact, everyone started doing Elvis, even around the office. How many times have you heard a fellow worker give the *Thank you. Thank you very much* line over some trivial favor?

I once went to a Dodger game with a friend. I thought it was just going to be baseball. But it was "Elvis night." Elvis songs were featured between innings, and numerous fans were decked out in Elvis regalia — fake sideburns and sunglasses and big black wigs.

And every time the JumboTron showed one of these ersatz Elvises, the crowd would go wild.

All these years after his death.

A true American original, Elvis. Yeah, you kind of have to overlook the years he made such masterpieces as *Harum Scarum* and *Change of Habit.* And we all know his last years were not happy ones, on the concert stage or in his personal life.

But early on, moving and shaking, all that energy and appeal and singing ability, that was the true Elvis. The Elvis who amazed Sam Phillips and blew away Roy Orbison, not to mention sixty million viewers of the *Ed Sullivan Show.* The Elvis poignantly recaptured in his 1968 "comeback" special.

There are no guarantees in the arts. But the ones who make it big usually do so by finding that spark of originality within them, that certain passion that ignites their creativity — and then wed that to a practical look at the commercial marketplace.

You want to sell? You have to do both. When you write, you should feel a little like 50's Elvis. Shake it, go for broke. Give freedom to your voice and your vision, the twins that make up the definition of originality. As Elvis put it in a 1956 interview, "Some people tap their feet, some people snap their fingers, and some people sway back and forth. I just sorta do 'em all together, I guess." To break through, you have to find out what it is you do well "together," and do it for all it's worth.

But you also need a little "Colonel" Tom Parker in you, and get wise to the markets.

It's an ongoing balancing act. You must never let your desire to be published completely drain you of your spirit and singularity (your inner Elvis).

But if you want to be published by someone other than Kinko's, you need market sense, too.

Don't be cruel. It's now or never.

Shake it, write it, sell it.

Action Scenes

Some time ago I participated in a panel discussion with some fellow thriller writers. During the Q & A we got this question from the floor: How can I learn to write a good action scene?

I answered first. I told the questioner that it's what happens *inside* the character that's the key, and you can make that implicit or explicit by using all the elements of fiction writing ---- dialogue, internal thoughts, description and action.

I recommended he read how Dean Koontz does it, especially in what is considered his breakout bestseller, *Whispers* (1980). There Koontz has an action scene (an attempted rape) that lasts 17 pages (that's right, 17 pages!)

all taking place within the close confines of a house.
Another panelist protested (in a good natured and
professional manner). He said action needs to be "realistic."
For instance, when a gunshot is fired nobody has time to
think. It all happens too fast. If they're shot, the pain
comes, and they will not be reflecting on anything. They'll
just be in pain.

Now this was grist for a great discussion. I licked my
chops but, unfortunately, we were at the very end of the
panel and time was called. I never got a chance to respond.
Now I do.

I would have said, first, that a gunshot does not cover the
wide spectrum of action. In the Koontz scene from
Whispers we have someone stalking the Lead. No guns. So
that example is of limited value.

But further, and even more important: fiction is not reality!
Fiction is the *stylized rendition* of reality for an *emotional
effect*.

That's so important I'll say it again: Fiction is the stylized
rendition of reality for an emotional effect.

Reality is boring. Reality is not drama. Reality is to be
avoided at all costs ("We must stay drunk on writing," Ray
Bradbury once said, "so reality does not destroy us.")

Hitchcock's Axiom holds that a great story is life *with the
dull parts taken out*. Reality has dull parts. Lots of them.

Fiction, if it works, does not.

A thriller writer wants the reader to believe he or she is
vicariously experiencing the story. We use techniques to
engage the reader's emotions all along the way. If there is

no emotional hook, there is no thrill, no matter how "real" the writing seems.

Let's have a look at a couple of clips from *Whispers*. Hilary Thomas, a successful screenwriter, comes home to discover that Bruno Frye, someone she'd met once, is waiting for her, and not for a game of cribbage.

> *She cleared her throat nervously. "What are you doing here?"*
> *"Came to see you."*
> *"Why?"*
> *"Just had to see you again."*
> *"About what?"*
> *He was still grinning. He had a tense, predatory look. His was the smile of the wolf just before it closed its hungry jaws on the cornered rabbit.*

Koontz breaks into the dialogue exchange for some description. The effect is like slow motion, which is another key to a good action scene. In essence, you slow down "real time" to create the feeling and tone you desire.

> *He took a step toward her.*
> *She knew then, beyond doubt, what he wanted. But it was crazy, unthinkable. Why would a wealthy man of his high social position travel hundreds of miles to risk his fortune, reputation, and freedom for one brief violent moment of forced sex?*

Now Koontz inserts a thought. In real time, when a rapist takes a step toward a victim, there would probably be no reflection, no pondering. But fiction *enhances* moments like this. Koontz is stretching the tension. He wants the reader taut while furiously flipping pages.

But 17 of them? Is Koontz insane? Or is he one of the best

selling writers in history for a reason?

In fact, Koontz is a consummate pro who knows exactly what he's doing. He even names it a couple of pages in:

Abruptly, the world was a slow-motion movie. Each second seemed like a minute. She watched him approach as if he were a creature in a nightmare, as if the atmosphere had suddenly become thick as syrup.

That, my friends, is stylized action for an emotional effect. If you'd like to grumble about that -- complain that it isn't "like reality" -- you may send your objections directly to Dean Koontz, who gives his address in the back of his books.

Let me know what he says.

Meanwhile, if you're looking to sell your fiction, learn to use the tools. Especially in actions scenes.

A Solid Bridge

Think of novel structure as a suspension bridge.

As is obvious from the picture, the suspension bridge is held up primarily by the two supporting pylons, one near the beginning of the bridge and one near the end. Without these pylons in those exact spots, the bridge will not be stable.

Now looking at the picture you can see that it perfectly represents the 3 act structure. A solidly constructed novel will look just like a solidly constructed suspension bridge. If that first pylon is placed too far out from the beginning, the first "act" of the bridge will sag and sway. In a book or movie, it means the first act is starting to drag.

Similarly, if the second pylon is misplaced, you'll end up either with anti-climax (the pylon too far away from the shore) or a feeling of *deus ex machina* (the pylon too close).

In my book, *Plot & Structure,* I refer to these pylons as "doorways of no return." I wanted to convey the idea of being forced through doorways, and once that's done, you can't go back again. Life will never be the same for the Lead. If you don't have that feeling in your story, the stakes aren't high enough.

Now, the first doorway is an event that thrusts the Lead into the conflict of Act 2. It is *not,* and this is crucial, just a decision to go looking around in the "dark world" (to use mythic terms). That's weak. That's not being forced.

A good example of a first doorway is when Luke Skywalker's aunt and uncle are murdered by the forces of the Empire in *Star Wars.* That compels Luke to leave his home planet and seek to become a Jedi, to fight the evil forces. If the murders didn't happen, Luke would have stayed on his planet as a farmer. He had to be forced out.

In *Gone With the Wind* it's the outbreak of the Civil War. Hard to miss that one. No one can go back again to the way things were. Scarlett O'Hara is going to be forced to deal with life in a way she never wanted or anticipated.

In *The Wizard of Oz*, it's the twister (hint: if a movie changed from black and white to color, odds are you've passed through the first doorway of no return).

In *The Fugitive*, the first doorway is the train wreck that enables Richard Kimble to escape, a long sequence that ends at the 30 minute mark (perfect structure) and has U. S. Marshal Sam Gerard declaring, "Your fugitive's name is Dr. Richard Kimble. Go get him!"

The second doorway, the one that closes Act 2 and leads to Act 3, is a bit more malleable, but just as critical. It is a clue or discovery, or set-back or crisis, one which makes *inevitable* the final battle of Act 3. It is the doorway that *makes an ending possible*. Without this, the novel could go on forever (and some seem to for lack of this act break).

In *The Fugitive,* at the 90 minute mark (the right placement for a film of just over two hours), Kimble breaks into the one-armed man's house and finds the key evidence linking him with the pharmaceutical company. This clue leads to the inevitable showdown with the "behind the scenes" villain.

In *High Noon*, the town marshal reaches the major crisis: he finally realizes no one in the town is going to help him fight the bad guys. That forces him into the final battle of Act 3, the showdown with the four killers.

By the way, this structure works for both "plot driven" and "character driven" stories. It's just that the former is mainly about outside events, and the latter about the inner journey. But that's beyond the scope of this post.

Now, there is always some well meaning literary genius howling in protest at the idea of structure. Too rigid! I don't write by formula! I am a rule breaker, a rebel! An artist! Away with your blueprints and let me run free! The 3 act structure is dead!

Let me say, first, I understand this artistic impulse. A good writer *is* a rebel, someone out to make waves.

But let me also say that the literary waters are littered with the works of those who ignored the basic principles of the suspension bridge. Unreadable novels with pretty words that didn't sell.

You want to write an experimental novel? Go for it. Just be aware that not a whole lot of people are going to care.

What they care about are characters, dealing with trouble by fighting their way over a bridge — meaning, through a plot that matters and is laid out in the right way.

Structure is "translation software" for your imagination. You've got a great story in your head. The characters, the feeling, the tone, the gut appeal, the *thing you want to say*. But it means squat unless you can share it with other people, namely, readers.

Structure allows you to get your story out with the greatest possible impact.

"But that's formulaic!" Well guess what, Skippy: formulas are formulas because they *work*. Try making an omelet out of Elmer's glue. What you, the writer, need to do is get people so caught up in the characters and stakes that they *can't see* the structure.

Many, if not most, published authors know this instinctively. But if there are problems with the novels, they may not always know where to look.

Consider Your Worth: Structure Analysis

1. Analyze the first act of your novel. Can you tell where the first doorway is? Is it an event that forces the Lead through, or is it softer, like a "decision"? Can you make it stronger?

2. Look at your second act. Is the action related to the story question set up in Act 1? In other words, your Lead has been forced into Act 2, so the action should relate to what got him there.

3. Can you identify a clue or discovery, or crisis or setback, that makes Act 3 possible?

4. Make the first act irresistible, the last act short, and everything in between compelling. Have you done that?

5. Hitchcock's Axiom states that a great story is life, with the dull parts taken out. So go through and take out all the dull parts: scenes with no real conflict or tension. You'll be making a stronger bridge as a result.

Need a Check Up?

My new doctor is young and aggressive. When I met him the first time he said he wanted to put me through a battery of tests, including a look at my ticker.

I said, "But Doc, I'm the picture of health!"

He did not care what I thought of my own pictures. He went on looking at my records, telling me I needed an updated this and a new that, then ordered that I get probed, scanned, tested, stuck and bled.

And so I was.

Some time later I got a message to call his office.

Now, when you get such a message you have a moment of panic. You start hearing those movie lines, you know, where the doctor says, "You have six months, maybe a year."

Or you wonder if he's going to want you in for full on heart surgery, today. (My response is that, in lieu of surgery, I'd prefer he just touch up the X-Rays).

Well, the news was all good. A clean bill of health.

But it got me to thinking. There are times in a writer's life when the pallor of impending doom falls over a manuscript. You think, Man, this thing is having heart problems. It's struggling for breath. I hope it isn't going to be DOA when it's finished!
I suggest in that instance you run some of your own tests. Like these:

THE HEAD

Step back and analyze: Is the Lead's objective strong enough? Readers want to care about a character's quest. Unless it is of absolutely vital importance to her well being, the objective is not going to grab the reader as it should. And by vital importance I mean that death is on the line—physical, psychological or professional. It can even be all three. (I have a section on the importance of "Death Overhanging" in *Revision & Self-Editing*).

THE LUNGS

The living, breathing center of your novel is the Lead character. Is he original, complex and in some very real way, compelling? Readers want a character who is not just some retread out of previous movies and books. You have to personalize and truly fall in love with the Lead. Here are two questions to ask: Do you find yourself thinking about the Lead even when you're away from the manuscript? Can you imagine your Lead living a life outside the book? If your answers are no, you need to do some deepening.

THE HEART

What is the "passionate center" of this novel for you? Have you lost it? Is your daily writing a dry exercise? Stop and write yourself a short letter. Pour out all your emotions. Be honest with yourself about the book. Here's the thing: you need to find out if you're writing only to sell. If so, you're more market driven than story driven. You're not being true to the tale trying to break out. And it will show. Manuscripts without heart are piled high in countless offices in New York.

Yes, selling is good and market considerations are wise. But they are *not enough* in today's competitive environment. What matters even more are the passion and individual voice you bring to the pages.

So give your story a check up in these areas and get your manuscript back to the health it so richly deserves.

Style Envy

Every writer, at one time or another, has what Freud called

style envy.

Or maybe it wasn't Freud. Maybe it was Gertrude Stein.

But I digress.

By style envy I mean we read things that make our jaws drop and our fingers ache. We think, *I could never write anything like that. I'm a fraud! Pay no attention to that man behind the curtain!*

I get style envy whenever I read Raymond Chandler. So many examples, like this from *Farewell, My Lovely:*

It was a blonde. A blonde to make a bishop kick a hole in a stained glass window.

Or from his short story "Red Wind":

There was a desert wind blowing that night. It was one of those hot dry Santa Anas that come down through the mountain passes and curl your hair and make your nerves jump and your skin itch. On nights like that every booze party ends in a fight. Meek little wives feel the edge of the carving knife and study their husbands' necks. Anything can happen. You can even get a full glass of beer at a cocktail lounge.

Or from *Playback:*

Mine was the better punch, but it didn't win the wrist watch, because at that moment an army mule kicked me square on the back of my brain. I went zooming out over a dark sea and exploded in a sheet of flame.

So what do you do about style envy? You remind yourself that every writer is different, and you too have a singular voice. Your duty is to develop that voice. Do that and you can sit back and enjoy great style without stress. Soak it up, and by osmosis you could be learning how to write what one of my favorite stylists, John D. MacDonald, called "unobtrusive poetry."

Here is MacDonald himself, from *Darker Than Amber*:

She sat up slowly, looked in turn at each of us, and her dark eyes were like twin entrances to two deep caves. Nothing lived in those caves. Maybe something had, once upon a time. There were piles of picked bones back in there, some scribbling on the walls, and some gray ash where the fires had been.

A new writer I met at a book signing, Steven M. Thomas, offers this in *Criminal Paradise*:

I caught a whiff of his body odor as he turned. He had slathered himself with cologne in lieu of bathing, but his scent penetrated the chemical astringency. He smelled like a neglected cage.
Style adds tone. Robert B. Parker is a master at this, as he shows in *Pale Kings and Princes*:

The sun that brief December day shone weakly through the west-facing window of Garrett Kingsley's office. It made a thin yellow oblong splash on his Persian carpet and gave up.
Do not neglect non-fiction writers. Rick Bragg is one of the best, as evidenced by this selection from *Ava's Man*:

She was old all my life. Even when I was sitting in the red dirt, fascinated with my own toes, Ava's face had a line in it for every hot mile she ever walked, for every fit she ever threw. Her hair was long and black as crows, streaked with white, and her eyes, behind the ancient, yellowed glass of her round spectacles, were pale, pale blue, almost silver. The blind have eyes like that, that color, but Ava could see fine, Ava could see forever. She could tell your fortune by gazing into the dregs of your coffee cup, and swore that if the bottoms of your feet itched, you would walk on strange ground. She could be gentle as a baby and sweet as divinity candy, but if her prescription was off, or if she just got mad, she would sit bolt upright in bed at three o'clock in the morning and dog-cuss anyone who came to mind, including the dead. Some days she would doze in her rocker and speak softly to people that I could not find, even by looking under the porch. Now I know I was just listening to her dreams.

Start a collection of great style, and read them over. Michael Connelly says he reads a certain chapter of Chandler's *The Little Sister* frequently. Seems to have worked for him.

Cool Papa Writing

I find it wonderfully ironic that I share the name of the man who many say was the fastest to ever play baseball.

Ironic, because speed afoot was never my gift, as it was for James "Cool Papa" Bell.

Another legend from the old Negro Leagues, Satchel Paige, was once asked just how fast Cool Papa was. Satch replied, "He can turn the light out and be in bed before the room gets dark."

Paige also asserted that Bell once hit a line drive off him, and the ball whistled past Paige's head and hit Bell in the buttocks as he slid into second base.

Now that's fast.

Bell was elected to the Baseball Hall of Fame in 1974.

So what does raw speed have to do with writing? Just this. When you write your first drafts, write as fast as you comfortably can. Even force yourself past the comfort zone on occasion. Whether you're an outliner, a seat-of-the-pantser, or anything in between, when you're getting those first pages down, burn rubber.

Why? Because there is so much good stuff in your writer's brain that needs to climb out of the basement and sniff the fresh air. You have to put your head down and butt the inner editor who stands at the basement door, telling you to be careful, slow down, don't make a fool of yourself.

It's also a way to just plain old get started when the "mountain" of the full novel looms ahead.

Write fast.

And lest someone sniff about how that only produces junk, consider:

-- William Faulkner wrote *As I Lay Dying* in six weeks, writing from midnight to 4 a.m., then sending it off to the publisher without changing a word.

-- Ernest Hemingway wrote what some consider his best novel, *The Sun Also Rises*, also in six weeks, part of it in Madrid, and the last of it in Paris, in 1925.

-- John D. MacDonald is now hailed as one of the best writers of the 1950's. Within one stunning stretch (1953-1954) he brought out seven novels, at least two of them – *The Neon Jungle* and *Cancel All Our Vows* –masterpieces. The others were merely splendid. Over the course of the decade he wrote many more superb novels, including the classic *The End of the Night*, which some mention in the same breath as Truman Capote's *In Cold Blood*.

So prolific was MacDonald that he was needled by a

fellow writer who, over martinis, sniffed that John should slow down, ignore "paperback drivel," and get to "a real novel." John sniffed back that in 30 days he could write a novel that would be published in hardback, serialized in the magazines, selected by a book club and turned into a movie. The other writer laughed and bet him $50 that he couldn't.

John went home and, in a month, wrote *The Executioners*. It was published in hardback by Simon & Schuster, serialized in a magazine, selected by a book club, and turned into the movie *Cape Fear*. Twice.

--Ray Bradbury famously wrote his classic *Fahrenheit 451* in nine days, on a rented typewriter. "I had a newborn child at home," he recalls, "and the house was loud with her cries of exaltation at being alive. I had no money for an office, and while wandering around UCLA I heard typing from the basement of Powell Library. I went to investigate and found a room with 12 typewriters that could be rented for 10 cents a half hour. So, exhilarated, I got a bag of dimes and settled into the room, and in nine days I spent $9.80 and wrote my story; in other words, it was a dime novel."

--Jack London was anything but promising as a young writer. He could hardly string sentences together in a rudimentary fashion. About all he had was desire. A burning desire. So he shut himself up in a room and wrote. Daily. Sometimes 18 hours a day. He sent stories off that got returned. He filled up a trunk with rejections. But all the time he was learning, learning. When he died at the age of 40 he was one of the most prolific and successful writers of all time.

It is in re-writing and editing that you slow down, cool off and shape what you've written. First drafts invariably need a lot of work. In re-write you deepen the prose and establish your style, sharpen your scenes and flesh out your characters. You can take your time here (with deadlines in mind, of course).

My own approach is to do my day's quota fast then spend time the next morning editing the pages before moving on. And once I do those edits, that's it till the end of the draft. As Satchel Paige said, "Don't look back, something may be gaining on you."

So when you first commit words to page, write fast. It helps you discover hidden "story stuff." This is especially important for newer writers. You learn most about writing a full length novel by actually writing a full length novel, and the sooner the better.

Write your first drafts like James "Cool Papa" Bell stealing second, then edit them like Satchel Paige, who took things slow and easy.

First Person Boring

I love a good First Person POV novel. I love writing FP myself. But there are perils, and if you're thinking of trying your hand at it you're going to need be aware of them.

One of these is the "I'm so interesting" opening that is anything but.

Recently I read a couple of novels in FP that had this problem. They began with the narrator telling us his name and giving us a chapter of backstory. By the time I finished the opening chapter I was thinking, Why am I even listening to you?

Let me illustrate. You go to a party and see a guy standing off to the side, you nod and introduce yourself, and he says, "Hi. My name is Chaddington Flesch. Most people call me Cutty, because my grandfather, Bill Flesch, refused to call me anything else. He liked Cutty Sark, you see, and thought this name would make a man out of me. All through school I had to explain why I was called Cutty. Growing up in Brooklyn, that wasn't always easy. Even today, at my job, which happens to be as an accountant, I . . ."

Yadda yadda yadda. And you're standing there at this party thinking, Dude, I'm sorry, but I don't especially care about your history. I have a history, everybody at this party has a history. Nice meeting you, but . . .

But what if you introduce yourself to the guy and he says, "Did you avoid the cops outside?"

You look confused.

"Because I got stopped by a cop right out there on the street. He tells me to hit the sidewalk, face down, and then proceeds to kick me in the ribs. I say, 'There's been a mistake.' He gets down in my face and says, 'You're the mistake. I'm the correction.'"

What are you thinking then? Either: *Am I talking to a criminal?* Or, *What happened to this poor guy?*

What your reaction *isn't* is *bored.*

You are hooked on what *happened* to him. And that's the key to opening with FP. Open with the narrator describing action and not dumping a pile of backstory.

Save that stuff for later.

Open with movement, with action.

I got off the plane at Maguire, and sent a telegram to my dad from the terminal before they loaded us into buses. Two days later, the Air Force made me a civilian, and I walked toward the gate in my own clothes, a suitcase in each hand.

I was a mess.

[361 by Donald Westlake]

The girl's name was Jean Dahl. That was all the information Miss Dennison had been able to pry out of her. Miss Dennison had finally come back to my office and advised me to talk to her. "She's very determined," my secretary said. "I just can't seem to get rid of her."

Then Miss Dennison winked. It was a dry, spinsterish, somewhat evil wink.

[*Blackmailer* by George Axelrod]

The nun hit me in the mouth and said, "Get out of my house."

[*Try Darkness* by James Scott Bell]

Now I realize I've used hardboiled examples here, and some of you favor more literary writing. There's a lot of debate on just how you define "literary," but let me suggest that literary does not mean *leisurely.* You can still open with a character in motion in a literary novel, and I guarantee you your chances of hooking an agent or editor, not to mention a reader, will go way up without any other effort at all.

One of my biggest tips to new writers is the "Chapter 2

Switcheroo." I can't tell you how many times I've looked at a manuscript and suggested that Chapter 1 be thrown out and Chapter 2 take over as the new opening. I would say, conservatively, that 90% of the time it makes all the difference, because the characters are *moving*. There's action. Something is happening. And truly important backstory can be dribbled in later. Readers will *always* wait patiently for backstory if your frontstory is *moving*.
Try it and see.

Hitting the Wall

My blog mate at Kill Zone, Michelle Gagnon, wrote a post on the "Fifty Page Mark," wherein she stated:

"I'm willing to bet that most of the people who never finish writing a book stall out right around that point, somewhere between 40-60 pages. And here's my theory as to why. After months or years of talking about writing a book (because at least as far as my experience at cocktail parties dictates, almost everyone believes they have a book in them), they've finally sat down and hammered some of those words on to the page! Initially, that's excitement enough. Because the outset is always thrilling. And things usually go swimmingly for ten to twenty pages. Then, something gets in the way--maybe they can't figure out what to tackle next in terms of the storyline, or their day to day life
intrudes."

I think there's a very good reason for this: Beginnings are easy. You've got this great idea. It's like falling in love. That may explain why getting those first 50 pages down seems like a joy. But then you face Act 2 and what, exactly, goes in there? That's the mountain, and I shudder at those who start scaling without the tools -- ropes, harnesses, even the right shoes. That is, at least a modest understanding of plot and scene construction. So I think you need to learn as you go: study the craft even as you write. And then finish the thing. You'll learn a lot just by finishing a draft. Then do it again. And again. And never stop.

Consider Your Worth: Follow Heinlein's Rules

Robert G. Heinlein, the great SF writer, said there are only two rules for writers:

1. You must write.

2. You must finish what you write.

So make sure you meet your weekly quota, whatever it is, until you're done. But also study the craft, as you're doing now, as much as you can at the same time.

Sex, Smells and Thrills

Sex is ever present. Drugs and Rock 'n Roll not as much. But since I write about fiction craft, I thought I'd offer opinions on the following topics:

Sex

I'm for it. I am married to a beautiful woman. But when it comes to literature and movies, a bit more nuanced thought is in order.

I realize there are certain types of lit where the "obligatory sex scene" (OSS) is expected. Erotica, some category romance, Barry Eisler books. But there, people know what they're getting.

In other fare, the OSS is very 1975. Back then it seemed that every movie had to have that sex scene, whether it made plot sense or not (e.g., *Three Days of the Condor*).

I'm against obligatory anything. If it doesn't make story sense, don't include it.

As far as explicit description, that may be showing its age, too. Renditions of body parts, insertions, ebbing, flowing, heaving, oceans, rivers, volcanoes, tigers, flames, conflagrations, arching backs, majestic canyons, verdant meadows of ecstasy, dewy vales of enchantment, flying and falling, flora and fauna and just about anything else involving motion, loss of breath, water metaphors and sweat seem, well, spent (oops, there's another one).

You know what works better? The reader's imagination. If you "close the door" but engage the imagination, it's often more effective than what you describe in words. Rhett carrying Scarlett up the stairs—do you need words to know exactly what happens?

One of the best sex scenes ever written is in *Madame Bovary*, the carriage ride with Emma and Leon (Part 3, Chapter 1 if you're interested). All the description is from the driver's POV, who cannot see into the carriage. Read it and see if you can do any better with body parts and a thesaurus.

Now, I do like well written sexual *tension*. That's a major theme in great fiction, especially noir and crime. So were the great 40's novels and films any less potent for not showing us what we know went on in the bedroom?

Smell

This is an underused sense in fiction, but quite powerful. Novelists are usually pretty good with sight and sound. But smell adds an extra something.

Rebecca McClanahan, in her fine book *Word Painting*, says, "Of the five senses, smell is the one with the best memory." It can create a mood quickly, vividly. Stephen King is a master at the use of smell to do "double duty" – that is, it describes and adds something to the story, be it tone or characterization.

In his story "All That You Love Will Be Carried Away," King has a middle aged salesman checking into yet another budget motel. His room, of course, has a certain look and smell, "the mingling of some harsh cleaning fluid and mildew on the shower curtain."

It is truly a smell that describes this guy's life.
Use smell properly in your fiction and it won't stink.

Thrills

For the writers here at Kill Zone, it's all supposed to add up to thrills. We have various techniques at our disposal for this, but we also know that clunky writing can pull you right out of our stories.

Or dumb things.

Like this recent movie I watched. I'm not going to name it, because I don't like to run down the other fella's product. Here's what happened. A brilliant detective is playing cat and mouse with a couple of killers who love the game. In the climactic scene, said detective has figured it out, and shows up at a remote location, gun drawn, telling the two killers to hold it! One killer has a gun, the other watches. Detective tells the one with the gun, who is on the brink of shooting someone, to put the gun down and walk over. So killer follows directions and puts the gun down . . . right where killer #2 can easily grab it!

Which he does. Not a cool move for the brilliant detective. But it was put in there so the rest of the scene could play out in thrilling fashion.

Only the thrill was gone, because the detective was so dumb.

Sex. Smell. Thrills. Use them wisely, my friends.

Consider Your Worth: Using Sex, Smell and Thrills

1. Sex. Do you feel like you have to include it? How explicitly? Try writing with sexual tension first. And then try "closing the door" on the, um, details. Show the *aftermath*. See if that doesn't work better for you . . . and for the reader.

2. Smell. Go through your manuscript. Choose the first scene, then five other key scenes. Work in a vivid smell into these places. Don't overdo it. Choose one good description that does "double duty" (adds to the tone or characterization) and leave it at that.

3. Thrills. Be especially careful about the "he/she wouldn't really" test. Does your character do anything dumb that causes more trouble? Cut those beats immediately. Pay close attention to the third act.

Ya Gotta Have Heart

Technique alone is never enough. You have to have passion. Technique alone is just an embroidered potholder. – Raymond

Chandler

John D. MacDonald wanted to bury the corpse. In this case, the corpse was one of his books. In 1963 he accepted an offer to write a novelization of a movie. The movie was Judy Garland's *I Could Go on Singing*. MacDonald took the gig because the money was good.

The book wasn't. Even he knew it. After it went out of print, MacDonald never gave permission for it to be printed again.

Since I collect MacDonald, I snagged a copy from a bookstore owner I know, who charged me a fair price. I did read it. And no, it isn't up to MacDonald's usual standards.
It's pretty obvious why: his heart wasn't in it. It wasn't his material.

Lesson: If you're going to get your writing noticed, read, published and re-read, you have to put your heart into it.

You've no doubt heard that before. At least once at every writer's conference, you'll hear someone on a panel say, "Forget chasing the market. Just write the book of your heart."

I understand what's being said, though I would tweak it a bit. You have to find the *intersection* of the market and your heart, then get that heart beating.

I'm a professional writer. I cannot afford to frolic in the fields of eccentric experimentation. But that doesn't mean I only write what I think will make money.

There are those who have done that. Nicholas Sparks is

right up front about how he chose his genre. He saw the tear-jerker-romance-by-a-male-author slot as a great business opportunity. David Morrell talks about this in his fine book, *Lessons From a Lifetime of Writing*. Morrell himself says he couldn't do it that way. He has to have something "gnawing" at him to write. He has to find the heart of the matter.

It's like when I was a criminal defense lawyer. (Spare me the jokes. When your son or daughter is arrested, you'll call someone like me.) Anyway, defense lawyers have an essential part to play in our system of justice. It's called upholding the Constitution. That's what you have to believe when you're defending someone who is pretty much cooked as far as the evidence goes. You have to believe that, or you'll do a lousy job.

I write for readers. I write so that readers will enjoy what I write and buy my next book. But to do that, I have to find the heart of the story and ramp up the passion level.

See, the unexpurgated "book of my heart" would be a post-realistic satirical look at the philosophy department of a major university, written somewhat in the style of Kurt Vonnegut channeling Jack Kerouac.
Could I sell such a book? I don't know. I know I'd enjoy writing it, but I also know it would be tough to sell a marketing department on it.

I could write it for fun, and might someday, but right now I need to keep earning a living.
So what I do is take my favorite genre, thrillers, think up concepts and then *make* them the book of my heart. I find ways to fall in love with my story.

The way it happens for me is through characters, getting to know them deeply, creating a colorful supporting cast --

and then scaring the living daylights out of them in the plot.

Synopsis Writing Made Easy

Every author I know hates writing a synopsis. They hate having to try to boil down their beloved story into 2 – 3 double spaced pages. They agonize over it, moan about it in public, throw fits, start the occasional bar fight. They would rather run in front of the bulls at Pamplona, wearing clogs, than write a short overview of their novel.

But don't buy your airline tickets to Spain just yet, because it's really not that hard. If you'll just follow these guidelines, you'll always have a solid synopsis, one you can show to any agent or editor and leave them wanting more.

A good synopsis is what I call "back cover copy on steroids." It's intended to "sell the sizzle" and give just enough of the steak to create confidence in the project.

This is not the same thing as a detailed outline, or treatment, which is much more substantial. The synopsis is a selling document. So approach it that way from the outset.

Before You Write the Synopsis

Build a foundation. Start from the ground up, one brick at a time.

Your first brick is a one sentence summary of your book. If you can't boil your book down into a single, compelling sentence, you are not ready to write it or sell it.

Second, expand that one sentence into back cover copy.

That's about 250 words of copy meant to sell your book to a harried consumer. You can easily learn to do this by getting books of similar genre from the library, or reading descriptions on amazon.com. Read a lot of these, studying the form. Write your own back cover copy. Work it until you have something that would make a consumer want to buy the book.

Now you're ready to write the synopsis.

The Parts of the Synopsis

1. The Opening paragraph
This tells us who the main character is, what he does (vocation), what he's like. Then one line on what the character wants at the present moment. A day before the story opens, what is the character going for? Goals? Drives?

Every Lead needs the above things. This first paragraph sets up the rest of the synopsis. Here's an example. (Note: The first time you introduce a character, use the full name and put it in ALL CAPS):

WALTER NEFF is a hotshot insurance salesman on the make for more business. He likes making money and having the occasional fling with women he makes house calls on. Even if they're married.

2. Second paragraph

The Disturbance. What is the incident that gets the story rolling?

One afternoon he calls on a client, and finds the client's wife, delicious blonde PHYLLIS DEITRICHSON, wrapped in a revealing towel from sunbathing. She gets

dressed and meets with him in the living room. During his pitch, Neff makes little comments about her looks and a game of sexual cat and mouse ensues. One thing for sure, when Walter Neff leaves the house he knows he's gone overboard for Mrs. Phyllis Deitrichson.

3. Basic plot paragraphs

Now you lay out the main plot, and I do mean *main*. The synopsis is not the place to detail all the subplots, though you should certainly mention them briefly. Write about them in a way that shows how they complicate the main plot. One or two paragraphs should be sufficient for this purpose.

You obviously have a lot of freedom here. You're going to be covering at least a page and a half with main plot material, the "sizzle" of the story. In the case of our example (obviously from the movie version of *Double Indemnity*) you'd stick to the plot to murder the husband and collect the insurance money, and the opposition represented by Barton Keyes, the sharp-eyed adjuster who can smell a scheme from miles away.

Walter comes in to work the next day, and sitting in the hallway the last man he wants to see—Jackson, the guy from the train who talked to him in the dark. Keyes has brought Jackson in because the account of the "accident" is starting to stink. Walter has to keep from being recognized as Jackson tells his story. Keyes slowly pulls in the net, though around whom he doesn't know yet. All he knows is that the "little man" inside him is raising Cain. And Walter knows all about how dangerous that little man is—to him and Phyllis.

4. Final Battle paragraph

Here you cover what I call the "final battle." It's the biggest crisis point your Lead character faces, what's at stake, why it's a battle to the "death." (It should at least feel that way to the character).

With Keyes closing in, Walter and Phyllis grow increasingly agitated. They try to meet in secret, but the strain begins to show. The seeds of distrust are sown. Then Walter discovers that Phyllis is seeing another lover. Now he must choose whether to run or take out his revenge — even if it sends him to the gas chamber.

5. Resolution
The last paragraphs (try to keep it to one or two) tell how the story ends.

Walter confronts Phyllis about her lover. Phyllis shoots Walter, wounding him, but can't finish the job. Running to his arms she states her love for him. He doesn't buy it. "Good-bye, baby," he says, then shoots her in the gut.

Losing blood, Walter dictates a confession to Keyes at the office late at night, then turns to see Keyes listening. Walter tries to get out, but doesn't make it past the front door. Keyes calmly calls the police.

And there you have it. A quick, easy guide to crafting a synopsis. Just remember:

• Don't try to tell everything, especially with regard to subplots.

• Aim for 2 – 3 pages, double spaced. If you go to four pages no one's going to arrest you, but you may be pulled over for holding up traffic.

• Rewrite and rewrite until it sounds like the marketing

copy on dust jackets and back covers of similar books. Give it to some faithful readers for feedback. Make sure they, and you, are jazzed by it.

• Send it out when requested, then wait for the offer to see the full manuscript. While you wait, be working on the synopsis of your next novel.

The Stress Free Query

The writing game is tough enough without stressing about minor things. Like how to structure a query.
"But," you shout, "a query is something worth stressing over, because there are four hundred things that can go wrong with it! I know, because I just read a blog titled 'The Four Hundred Most Common Query Mistakes.' So I have every reason to stress out!"

Okay, let's sit back in our chairs and take a nice, deep, relaxing breath. You would think from all that is out there that query writing is like the cave at the beginning of *Raiders of the Lost Ark.* You know, one false move and a dozen arrows ventilate you, or you get impaled by spikes, leaving you as a rotting carcass with no agent and no prospects.

Instead of focusing on all the things you can do wrong, why don't we just look at the simple basics of a query and how you can get them right—*every time?*

After the salutation which addresses the agent or editor by name (i.e., not *Dear Sir or Madam* or *To Whom it May Concern*), three paragraphs are all you need.

The Opening Paragraph

Your plot, starting with the Lead character's name:

[Lead character] is a [occupation or vocation] who [life situation].

Now write four to six lines which give the *ka-ching* factor of your plot. Write this paragraph as if it were a 30 second movie spot.

Here's an example taken from the back cover of *Side by Side* by TKZ's own John Ramsey Miller:

Winter Massey is a former U.S. marshal who has made too many enemies on both sides of the law. Lucy Dockery is a judge's daughter who's never had to fight for anything in her life. But now Lucy and her young son have been kidnapped and sentenced to die-unless her father agrees to set a vicious criminal free. Massey is the closest thing to salvation they have, but he doesn't know that the beautiful FBI agent who brought him into the case may be playing a chilling double game -- and that a circle of treachery has begun to tighten around him. For Lucy, the time has come to scratch and claw for survival. For Massey, it's time to stop trusting the people he trusts most. Because in a storm of betrayal, there's only one way out.

Train yourself to write this way be reading the back cover copy of books in your genre (or the editorial descriptions off amazon.com).

I advise starting off with the plot paragraph because you want to show the agent you can grab readers from the start. Most queries agents see start off with some meet-and-greet stuff. There's nothing really wrong with that, but since agents see this all the time, why not stand out from the crowd?

The Background Paragraph

Now give a paragraph with the title, genre, word count, and *relevant* parts of your background. Writing credits are good if they are "weighty" credits. By that I mean a reputable publication. Something a bit more than your local grocery store newsletter. It's better to err on the side of no credits than a string of flimsy ones. There's no hard rule here, just put yourself in the reader's place. Does it truly indicate anything about your writing chops? If you got an award or grant that's prestigious, or earned an MFA, by all means mention.

Experience in the field you're writing about is good. Where you were born and how much you love writing is not good. How well you think you'll do on TV interviews is horrible. Worst of all is saying your book is the "next" anything [James Patterson; *Harry Potter*] or is definitely going to be on the big screen as a major motion picture, and don't you, Ms. Agent, want to get in on that action?

Don't waste any time on how you came to write the story, what your grandmother and critique group think of it, or how you the publisher should market you.

If you had some interaction with the agent or editor at a conference, or heard them speak, or read something good on their blog, you can mention that. Briefly.

[*Title*] is a 95,000 word thriller. I've been a practicing lawyer for fourteen years. This is my first novel. I heard you speak at the Greater Downey Writers Conference and think this project would be a good fit for you.

And please, don't get cutesy with this paragraph, as in:

Your blog post on queries was almost as good as Dave Barry, LOL! He makes me laugh, you made me laugh, and I'm sure we'll have both a lot of laughs when that first contract comes in! ;-)

You get the idea. Here's why you don't have to stress about your bio. The thing that's going to sell you in the query is your plot paragraph. Let your background paragraph do its work and get out of the way.

The Thank You Paragraph

This is tricky:

Thank you for your consideration.

Then put your name and contact phone number.

Now that wasn't so hard, was it?

Since most queries are now electronic, and agents don't generally want attachments, put the query in the body of your email, using the default font and block paragraphs (no indents; single spaced). Put two spaces between the paragraphs.

The subject line should have QUERY in it. There have been reports of none-too-clever attempts to stand out from other emails by putting in fake headlines, e.g., *End of the World Clues Here!*

Don't do that. It's unprofessional. While it might not scuttle your chances of getting a request for you manuscript, it's a bit of a turnoff. Why make it harder on yourself?

There you go. No stress, no strain. Now you can

concentrate on your writing.

Garlic Breath, or What Not to Do on Your Opening Page

"If you cannot write a compelling opening scene, from the opening sentence, I'm not going to finish your proposal." – Agent, speaking at a recent writers conference

The opening page of your novel is your big introduction. It's what an agent will read with most interest, to see if you can write (which is why page 1 is often the *first* thing read in your proposal. You may have spent 100 hours on a killer synopsis, 50 on an irresistible query, but if the writing itself is not up to snuff, the busy agent can save time by tossing the whole thing aside without reading the rest of the proposal).

Think of it this way. You are at a party and the man or woman of your dreams is across the room. The host offers to introduce you. You walk over. There is great anticipation, even from Dreamboat, who is there to meet people, too. So Dreamboat extends a hand, you take it, and say, "Nice to meet you."
Only you have a horrendous case of garlic breath. Dreamboat winces, whips out a phone and walks quickly away, muttering, "I have to take this."

Well, that's what it's like for an agent reading your first page. He or she *wants* to like you, but if you've got garlic breath, it's all over. Bad first impression. See you later.

I taught at a writers conference recently, where attendees were invited to submit the opening page of their manuscripts – anonymously. We then put these on two transparencies. The first one as is, the second I had marked up as a tough editor might.

It was quite educational. I got 12 first pages in all, and none were ready for prime time. There were several items that should be *avoided at all costs* on the first page. Here they are, in no particular order:

Characters Alone, Thinking

This was in the majority of the first pages I reviewed. We did not get a scene, which is a *character in conflict with others in order to advance an agenda.* We got, instead, the ruminations of the character as he/she reflects on something that just happened, or the state of his/her life at the moment, or some strong emotion. The author, in a mistaken attempt to establish reader sympathy with the character, gave us static information.

Such a page is DOA, even if the character is "doing" something innocuous, like preparing breakfast:

Marge Inersha tried to mix the pancake batter, but thoughts of Carl kept swirling in her head, taking her mind off breakfast and back to Tuesday, horrible Tuesday when the sheriff had served her with the divorce papers. Tears fell into the batter, but Marge was powerless to stop them. She put the mixing bowl on the counter and wiped her eyes. How much more could she take? With two kids sleeping upstairs?

Marge is certainly hurting, but you know what? I don't care. I hate to be piggy about this, but I really don't care that Marge is crying into her pancake batter. The mistake writers make is in thinking that readers will have immediate sympathy for a person who is upset.

They won't. It's like sitting at a bar and guy next to you grabs your sleeve and immediately starts pouring out his troubles to you.

Sorry, buddy, I don't care. We all got troubles. What else is new?

Don't give us a character like that on page 1.

Dreams

Agents and editors hate it when you open with a dream. And so do most readers. Because if they get invested in a cool opening, and then discover it's all been a dream, they feel cheated. So you may have a gripping first page, but you'll ruin the effect when the character awakens.

Yes, I know some bestselling authors have done this. When you start selling a gazillion copies, you can do it, too. Until then, you can't.

Exposition Dump

In most of the first pages I reviewed there was entirely too much exposition. The author thinks that this is information the reader *has to know* in order to understand the character and the scene.
In truth, readers need to know very little to get into the story. They will wait a long time for explanations and backstory if the action is gripping, essential, tense or disturbing. My rule, ever since I began writing and teaching, is *act first, explain later.*

This rule will serve you amazingly well your entire writing career.

Weather Without Character

Another complaint you'll hear from editors and agents is about "weather openings." This is a catch all phrase for generic description. Chip MacGregor, agent, described his opening pet peeve this way: "The [adjective] [adjective] sun rose in the [adjective] [adjective] sky, shedding its [adjective] light across the [adjective] [adjective] [adjective] land."

If you're gong to describe weather on the opening page, make sure you've established a character on whom the weather is acting. And make sure that character is not alone, thinking.

Point of View Confusion

Another big error was a confusion about Point of View. This comes in several guises.

1. We don't have a strong POV character. Who does this scene belong to?

2. We "head hop" between different characters on the same page, losing focus.

3. We have the terrible sin of "collective POV." That is, we get a description of two or more characters who think or perceive the same thing at the same time.

John and Mary ran from the gang, wondering where they were going to go next.

The 300 Spartans turned and saw the Persians approaching.

4. We have First Person narration without a compelling voice. First Person needs attitude.

5. We don't have a POV at all until the second or third paragraph. We have description, but no idea who is perceiving it. We need that information right away.

So these are some very big *don't'* on your first page.

Consider Your Worth: Opening Page Don'ts

1. Look over your opening page. Do you find any of the above errors?

2. Re-write your opening page according to the principle of the disturbance, which is the next entry.

How to Grab Them on Page One

Now let's talk about an opening page strategy that works for any type of fiction.

At the outset, please note that what follows is *not* a formula. This isn't painting by the numbers. But it is a *principle*, and thus has infinite possibilities for application. No matter what your style or genre, this principle will work its magic for you, every time.

Recall that last week's post was triggered by something an agent said at a recent conference, to wit: "If you cannot write a compelling opening scene, from the opening sentence, I'm not going to finish your proposal."

I assume you do want agents -- and editors -- to finish your proposal. If so, you must grab them on page one. How can you do that?

By beginning your novel with a *disturbance to the Lead's ordinary world.*

Why disturbance? Because: Readers read to *worry*. They want to be lost in the intense emotional anticipation over the plight of a character in trouble. Only when that connection is made does reader interest truly kick in.

But in their opening pages many writers fall into what I call the "Happy people in Happy Land" trap. They think that by showing the Lead character in her normal life, being happy with her family or dog or whatever, we'll be all riled up when something bad happens to this nice person, perhaps at the end of chapter one, or beginning of chapter two.

Or they fall into the "I'm the Greatest Literary Stylist of Our Time" trap. This is where a writers desires to display brilliance via pure prose before, somewhere down the line, something like a plot kicks in.

But that's too long to wait. You need to stir up the waters immediately.

A disturbance is something that causes ripples in the placid lagoon of Happy Land. It can be anything, so long as it presents a change or challenge to the Lead. (It's important to note that this disturbance need not be "big" as in, say, a thriller prologue. The opening disturbance can be a jolt, however slight, that indicates to the Lead she is not having an ordinary moment here).

And you need to have that jolt on page one, preferably paragraph one.

This is true for both commercial and literary fiction, BTW. Compare the following two openings, the first a commercial example, the latter a literary one.

They threw me off the hay truck about noon.

(The Postman Always Rings Twice by James M. Cain)

The world outside the window was in flames. The leaves on the pistachio trees shone fire-red and orange. Mattie studied the early morning light. She was lying on the side of the bed where her husband should have been sleeping.

(*Blue Shoe* by Ann Lamott)

Notice that Cain starts with a character in motion at a point in time that is obviously a disturbance to him. In this case, the disturbance is physical.

In Lamott's example, we have two lines of description, then the Lead is introduced, and the last line is a ripple of disturbance, this one emotional: where is her husband?

Dialogue, if it indicates immediate conflict, is another way to create an opening disturbance. I've heard more than one agent say they like to see dialogue in the first pages. Why? Because it means you are writing a scene. Not exposition or description or backstory, but a real scene. Like this:

"The marvelous thing is that it's painless," he said. "That's how you know when it starts."
"Is it really?"
"Absolutely. I'm awfully sorry about the odor though. That must bother you."
"Don't! Please don't."

("The Snows of Kilimanjaro" by Ernest Hemingway)

From these examples it's plain to see that there are countless ways to grab readers right away through this wonderful thing called *disturbance.*

Now why wouldn't you want to do that?

Perhaps you have a reason. Maybe style is what you're

after most of all. A mood. Or maybe you're writing a grand epic, and want to "set the scene" as it were. But before you abandon the disturbance principle, look at the opening lines from a couple of "big" novels:

The boys came early to the hanging. (*The Pillars of the Earth*, Ken Follett)

The gale tore at him and he felt its bite deep within and he knew that if they did not make landfall in three days they would all be dead. (*Shogun*, James Clavell)

I don't know about you, but that's enough narrative energy to propel me through the next few pages. If I get a long weather report up top, or two pages on the sunlight over Rio (no matter how beautifully rendered) I will be sorely tempted to put the book down. If you tell me how the character got to the scene, via backstory or flashback, I'm definitely moving on.

But if you indicate there's a character here facing change or challenge, uncertainty or conflict, I'm going to want to know why. I don't need to know the background info yet. I'll wait for that if trouble is brewing.

John LeCarre once said, "*The cat sat on the mat* is not the opening of a plot. *The cat sat on the dog's mat* is."

Mr. LeCarre has it right. The opening page of a novel has to draw the reader in with an indication of trouble to come.

Do that by disturbing your characters from the very start.

Death to Prologues?

"First thing we do, let's kill all the prologues." -- Shakespeare (hack writer Chip Shakespeare of Schenectady, NY)

Every now and then a new "fiction rule" begins to get trumpeted about until it gets chiseled in a tablet as an unbreakable command. Here's one that seems to be developing: No prologues!

You hear this occasionally from agents and even readers. So it behooves us to ask if there's something to this mushrooming new "rule."

I think there is--and isn't.

Let me explain.

First, a definition. A prologue is a scene (or sometimes a group of scenes) that precedes in time the main plot. So the question to ask yourself is, if it isn't part of the main plot, why am I including it? And why should a reader bother with it?

Some reasons you might include a prologue:

• To start the book with intense action that hooks the reader.

• To set up an intriguing mystery that will pay off later in the book.

• To show a significant incident in the Lead's life that haunts him in the present.

• To demonstrate the evil deeds of the bad guy, setting up the stakes for the Lead.

What a prologue should not be is merely an excuse to give us backstory, the sort of information about the Lead that can wait to be revealed later. Only if the material in the prologue is absolutely essential, riveting and has real impact on the story, should it be used.

Maybe that's why agents are suspicious. They see too many prologues that don't need to be there.

Some readers report that they skip prologues. Why would they do that? Perhaps because it seems to them that it's just setup information and they want to get right on to the story.

So what should you do if you've got a great prologue that makes sense? That accomplishes just what it's suppose to?

Should you give up and bow to the blanket rule that you should never use a prologue? I don't think so.

Instead, be deceptive.

That's right. I said deceptive. You're a fiction writer, after all. That's what you do.

So here is a simple strategy: never label a prologue as "Prologue." That's an invitation for a reader, not to mention an agent or editor, to skip this part or toss aside the manuscript.

Instead, if it's in the long past, you can start with a date stamp, like this:

November 22, 1963

Or you can simply decide to call it "Chapter One."

Another option is simply not to put anything at all. I like this move. You just go halfway down the page and start your scene. Then, you can number the next scene as Chapter One. This was the strategy used by Harlan Coben in *Tell No One*. There is no call out that the book opens with a prologue. It simply gives us a riveting scene about a husband losing his wife and getting knocked out. Then, the next scene is headed:

1
Eight Years Later

But Coben wrote such a great opening scene that you don't stop and say, "Hey! He fooled me! That was a prologue! I want my money back!"

So here's my bottom line advice. Don't start with a prologue unless you have an absolutely clear reason for doing so. Make it short, too, unless you can justify the longer opening--as in, say, *Mystic River*, where the opening scenes, in the long past, are essential to understanding the plot as it unfolds. Dennis Lehane knew what he was doing.
Make sure you do, too, and then just don't call it a "Prologue." Problem solved.

What About the Semi-Colon?

When it comes to fiction writing, I think of semi-colons the way I think of eggplant: avoid at all costs. As Kurt Vonnegut once said, "Here is a lesson in creative writing. First rule: Do not use semicolons ... All they do is show you've been to college."

The semi-colon is a burp, a hiccup. It's a drunk staggering

out of the saloon at 2 a.m., grabbing your lapels on the way and asking you to listen to one more story.

Not that I have an opinion, you understand.

Okay, I'll modify things a bit. For non-fiction, essays and scholarly writing, the semi-colon does serve a purpose; I've used them myself. In such writings you're often stringing two thoughts together for a larger point, and the semi-colon allows you to clue the reader in on this move.

But in fiction, you want each sentence to stand on its own, boldly. The semi-colon is an invitation to pause, to think twice, to look around in different directions, to wonder where the heck you're standing. Do you want that? Or do you want your story to *move?*

The semi-colon is a stone that causes the reader to stumble.

Not that they'll notice this on a conscious level. Most won't think, "Why'd he use a semi-colon here? I'm being taken out of the story!" No, but it will have that very effect, on a subconscious level. It will weaken the reading experience in a small way. Not fatally, but why would you want even a small speed bump in your story?

The semi-colon is especially grating in dialogue:

"We must run to the fire," Mary said. "It is going to burn the town; that is a disaster!"

What's that semi-colon doing there? Is it making Mary's dialogue stronger or weaker? Is it adding to the intensity of the moment or diluting it?

Semi-colons. For academics, yes. For novelists, no.

How to Write Your Last Page

There's more than enough material on how to open a book, first pages and so on.

But what about your last page?
I love the Mickey Spillane quote: "The first page sells your book. The last page sells your *next* book."

How true that is. How many times have we begun a novel or movie, only to be let down when the book is closed or the credits roll?

I love beginnings. Beginnings are easy. I can write grabber beginnings all day long. So, I suspect, can you.

But endings? Those are hard.

Why? First, because with each passing day another book or movie has come out, another ending has been rendered. So many great endings have already shown up. We who continue to write have the burden of trying to provide satisfactory surprise at the end when so much ending material is already out there.

Second, our endings have to tie things up in a way that makes sense but is also unanticipated. If the reader can see it from a mile away, the effect is lost.

I like what Boston University writing teacher Leslie Epstein said in a recent *Writer's Digest* piece ("Tips for Writing and for Life," WD March/April 2010). When asked if a writer must know the ending before he starts, Epstein says, "The answer is easy: yes and no. One must have in mind between 68 and 73 percent of the ending."

Epstein's having a bit of fun here, but his point is solid. If you have the ending 100% in mind, you're in a straitjacket, unable to let your story sufficiently breathe, or twist, or turn.

On the other hand, if you don't have any idea where you're going, you could easily fall into the meander trap, or the backed-into-a-corner trap.

I want to offer you my own personal approach to writing endings. It's called *Stew, Brew and Do*.

Why is it called that? Because I made it up so I get to name it.

Here's how it goes:

Step 1: Stew.

I spend a lot of time at the end of a manuscript just stewing about the ending. Brooding over it. I've got my final scenes in mind, of course, and have written toward them. I may even have written a temporary ending. But I know I won't be satisfied until I give the whole thing time to simmer. I put the manuscript aside for awhile, work on other projects, let the "boys in the basement" take over.

I tell myself to dream about the ending before going to bed. I write down notes in the morning.

Step 2: Brew.

When I am approaching the drop dead deadline, I continue to outline ending possibilities. I will have files of notes and ideas floating in my head. When I know I have to finish I use *Brew* in both a practical and metaphorical way.

I take a long walk. There is a Starbucks half an hour from my office. (In fact, there is a Starbucks half an hour from anyplace in the world). I put a small notebook in my back pocket and walk there and order a brew—a solo espresso. I down it, wait a few minutes and then start writing notes in the notebook. Then I walk another half an hour, to another Starbucks (I'm not kidding). There I make more notes. If I have to, I have another espresso. I am a wild-eyed eccentric at this point, but I do have ideas popping up all over the place.

Step 3: Do.

I go back to my office and write until finished.

Well, it works for me. I like most of my endings, but they were very hard work to get to. But hey, that's good. If this gig was easy, everybody'd be doing it, right?

The Great Italics Controversy

I love the way writing "rules" sometimes get floated around the internet, become a meme, then move to "accepted wisdom" or even "non-negotiable truths from on high" – while, all along, it may just be the wrong for an across the board regulation.

That's how it is these days with italics, especially when used for rendering the inner thoughts of a character. You know how that's often done:

Susan walked into the room and saw Blake. *Back in town! I don't want him to see me like this!*

That's the shortest possible route to showing us the inner

thought. Another alternative is to not use italics, but put in an attribution:

Susan walked into the room and saw Blake. Back in town, she thought. I don't want him to see me like this!

A third way is to use 3d Person, but filtered in such a way that we know it is Susan thinking it.

Susan walked into the room and saw Blake. So he was back in town. She didn't want him to see her like this.

That last two renderings are probably the preferred type these days. Or at least the fashion cops seem to think so. But does that mean italics should never be used for thoughts?

Never say never, especially when it comes to writing "rules." I think italics are still perfectly acceptable when used in moderation.

Note that word: moderation. The overuse of italicized thoughts gets a bit wearying.

But an italicized thought may be the best, most economical way for a character to recall a key point or phrase uttered earlier in the book. And to set it off for the reader, too.

For example, early in the book your Lead character is given a clue about the villain by someone, who says, "Baxter will be wearing cheapie shoes that squeak."

Near the end of the book, the character hears someone enter the room with squeaky shoes. You could write it the clunky way: **She listened to the sound of his shoes on the tile. And she remembered what Clive had told her about Baxter, that he would be wearing inexpensive shoes that**

squeak.

Or you could do it quickly and easily with italics:

She listened to the sound of his shoes on the tile.
Baxter will be wearing cheapie shoes that squeak . . .

If you have a scene that is mostly interior dialogue, using italics can be a means of variety. In Lisa Scottoline's *Courting Trouble,* lawyer Anne Murphy has to process some shattering news. First, Scottoline uses no italics:

Could this be? Could this really be? Was Willa dead? Anne's heart stalled in her chest. Her eyes welled up suddenly, blurring the busy boardwalk . . . . She struggled against the voice and the conclusion, but she couldn't help it. Willa, dead? No!

But then, as Anne continues to try to "wrap her mind" around it, there's this:

Kevin got out, but how? Why didn't they tell her?

The switch to italics, for one line, adds a certain immediacy to the thought process. I don't think Scottoline should be arrested for using it. I don't even think she should get a ticket.

In *The Hard Way* by Lee Child, a man in a hooded sweatshirt who takes money off drunks is walking down the street, and sees: **A big man, but inert. His limbs were relaxed in sleep.**

As the hooded man moves closer, Child inserts a series of quick thoughts, between paragraphs of narrative:

His hair was clean. He wasn't malnourished.

Not a bum with a pair of stolen shoes.
[more narrative]
A prime target.

And so on. It's just an efficient way to get the point across and get out of the way. Could the same thing be done without italics? Perhaps. Should it? That's up to you. Another Jab against Italics Is that they are "hard to read." I don't buy that. That's why I didn't mind that Robert Crais has whole chapters in italics in *L.A. Requiem.* He has a reason for it, and I'm not going to call the Style Felony Hotline to report him.

Here's my pragmatic conclusion: yes, there may be some prejudice against italics forming. But if they're used quickly for a good reason, I see no problem.

One Plus One Equals Three

"I've always believed the greatest rock and roll musicians are desperate men. You've got to have something bothering you all the time. My songs are good because ... it's like in art and love, hey, one and one makes three. In music, if it makes two, you've failed, my friends. You know, if you're painting, if all you've got is your paint and your canvas, you've failed. If all you got is your notes, you've failed. You've got to find that third thing that you don't completely understand, but that is truly coming up from inside of you. And you can set it any place, you can choose any type of character, but if you don't reach down and touch that thing, then you're just not gonna have anything to say, and it's not gonna feel like it has life and breath in it, you're not gonna create something real, and it's not gonna feel authentic. So I worked hard on those things." – Bruce Springsteen

We need to get that. Your book, if it's going to go anywhere, has to be about more than what it is about. It has to dig deep somewhere, so the readers think there's a "there" there, something the author really cares about.

An "inner ferret," as grandmaster thriller author David Morrell puts it. Others might call it heart. Still others, like the late great Red Smith, say, "Just open a vein."

But your novel should be something that moves your insides around.

How do you find it?

Start making a list. Make a list of things that bother you, that get your juices flowing. I often ask writing students what is something that would make them throw a chair out the window? Write about that thing. Put that feeling inside your Lead character.

Or make a list of memories that are vivid to you. Why are they vivid? Because your subconscious is trying to tell you something. Find that thing.

Ray Bradbury started making a list of nouns of remembrance when he was young. He came up with nouns like THE LAKE, THE CRICKETS, THE SKELETON, THE NIGHT, and so on. Each one of these referred to something from his childhood. He went into those memories and mined them for stories.

Childhood fears seem to play a big role not only for Bradbury, but also King and Koontz. Figuring out why justice is worth going for in a world that seems dead set against it animates Michael Connelly . . . and me. That seems to be a consistent thread throughout my novels.

Maybe that's because I was brought up by a dad who was an L.A. lawyer who often represented the poor accused of crimes. He had a passion for the Constitution and criminal justice. I guess I absorbed that.

So what about you? Is there some "inner ferret" that drives your writing? What equals three for you? Find out. Nurture it. Use it. Write it.

Consider Your Worth: Make a List

1. Start a list for yourself. Nouns, like Bradbury. Add to it periodically.

2. What things would you fight for?

3. What things would you die for?

4. What are the five most important issues in life for you?

5. Write about these things!

How Many Subplots is Too Many?

Someone asked a question on Twitter: *How many subplots is too many?*

At first, I was going to say something profound like, "That depends." But then I started to noodle on it, and decided what we need here is a formula.

My tongue is planted only slightly in my cheek here, because the more I think about it, the more I think this formula actually works. If there's going to be an exception, you'll have to justify it. But if you stick to these parameters, I think you'll be fine.

First, what is a subplot? It's a plot line that has it's own story question and arc. It usually complicates the main plot in some way. It may or may not involve the same Lead character as in the main plot.

A subplot is not merely a plot "complication." A subplot has its own reason for being, and weaves in and out of (or back and forth with) the main plot. Or it might go along on its own until it links up with the main later in the book. But here's the deal: because it does have its own reason for being, it's going to take up a significant chunk of real estate in your novel.

That being so, here is my formula for the maximum number of subplots, by word count, you can have in your novel (a novel being a minimum of 60,000 words).

60k words: 1 subplot (e.g., in a category romance, you might have the female Lead plotline, and the love interest plotline, which intersect)

80k: 2-3

100k: 3-4

Over 100 k: 5

There is no 6. Six subplots is too many for any length, unless your name is Stephen King.

If you have more subplots than suggested above, they will tend to overwhelm or detract from the main plot.

The First Line Game

A number of my novelist friends share an e-mail loop, and from time to time we put up the first lines of our WIPs. It's always fun to strut our stuff and see what others are doing.

First lines can also be an idea generator. Dean Koontz, in his book *How to Write Best Selling Fiction* (1981), told how he used to do this all the time, in order to find material. One day he wrote this:

"You ever killed anything?" Roy asked.

He stared at it awhile, then decided Roy was fourteen and talking to a younger boy. And from that one line he developed what became *The Voice of the Night*.

Joseph Heller wrote this line, without knowing anything else: *In the office in which I work there are five people of whom I am afraid.* This became the genesis of his massive satirical novel, *Something Happened.* (The line was moved further in by Heller once the book was finished, but it was the line itself that suggested the larger work).

I was at Bouchercon last week, in a good place because I had just submitted my manuscript to my editor. I am about to begin another novel, so sitting in the hotel lobby one afternoon, I was "in between." I took out my notebook and wrote this line:

He had loved her since she was six years old.

Now, that is not my usual style, and it has the word *had* in it, which I would normally try to eschew. But that's what I wrote. Then I kept on writing, to find out what the scene was about. When I got to the end of the page I had made two startling discoveries, both of which I'll keep to myself as I may actually want to write this thing!

It is very cool to find ideas this way. Do you ever do that?

Try it!

Consider Your Worth: You Opening Line

1. Spend an hour just writing first lines. Use a dictionary: open, at random, to a word, and do a first line based on it.

2. Pick your top three.

3. Tweak them.

4. Pick your favorite one, and write a scene based on the line. Don't plan the scene, let it happen as you write.

5. Assess. Develop the idea further if you like it. Or go back to another and follow step 4 again.

Before You Submit

The May/June 2010 issue of *Writer's Digest* has a sidebar from YA editor Anica Morse Rissi, wherein she gives nine things you can do to elevate your manuscript before submission.

I thought the list was good. Not only for getting a manuscript ready to submit to agents or editors, but also if you're considering self-publishing. So I'm going to give you the tips with my own comments attached.

1. Revise, revise, revise.

As the author of a whole book on the revision process, I'm not going to quibble with this one. You can, however, become "revision obsessed" and spend way too long on a project. In my book I give a process for getting over that, but you can just as well come up with one of your own, so long as you eventually send your work out. Not too soon, but not too late, either.

2. Start with conflict and tension.

This is perhaps the most important tip of all. Some of our highest traffic here at TKZ has come from posts on what to do -- and what not to do -- on first pages, as well as the numerous first page critiques we've done. Search those out in the archives. Now, conflict or tension does not have to be "big." It can really be any sort of disturbance to the Lead's ordinary world.

3. Don't start with backstory.

An obvious corollary to #2. Backstory is best when it is delayed, although little sprinkles can be added to the first pages for depth. Just make the action primary up front.

4. Give the readers something to wonder about.

Mystery, unanswered questions, portents, threats. All good at the beginning and, indeed, throughout — so long as you are prepared to give satisfactory answers (unless you write for *Lost*, of course, then you can just keep on raising questions).

5. Avoid explaining too much, too soon.

A corollary to #4. My rule for the opening is *act first,*

explain later. Readers do not need to know everything you do about the setting and characters at the start. They will wait a long time if there's something dynamic and disturbing going on at the beginning.

6. Make sure your story has plot arc and emotional arc.

This is another way of saying that you need to give us the stakes inside the character, as well as outside. One way to do this is via internal conflict, which is the battle between two strong but opposing desires in the character. In *High Noon*, the town marshal must battle his desire to do his duty as a lawman versus his desire to keep his new Quaker bride (the producers raise the stakes nicely by having the Quaker bride look exactly like Grace Kelly).

7. Read your dialogue out loud.

This is a great practice. You hear it differently than you read it. An alternative (my own preference) is to have Word read it back to me in speech mode. Either way, you'll catch things to change every time.

8. Use adjectives, adverbs and dialogue tags sparingly.

As far as adverbs, do a search for LY words and kill as many of those pests as you can. For dialogue tags, use *said* and *asked* as your defaults, and only when needed to figure out who's speaking. Resist the urge to use things like *he growled* or *he expostulated.*

9. Make sure your details matter.

All details, and I mean every one in your manuscript, should do "double duty." Not just describe, but describe in a way that sets the tone you desire. Details can characterize, foreshadow and carry motifs. In other words, don't waste them.

To these fine suggestions, I would also add the following (from my chapter on "The Polish")—go over each chapter and see how much you can cut from the beginning and the end. You'll be amazed at how much faster your chapters grab, and how you'll be left with a feeling of momentum ɒftɒr ɒnɒh ɒɒɒnɒ.

Just Go

I love writing about the craft of fiction. I love it because I had to teach myself how to write back when I was being told writing could not be learned. I had come to believe that (about 90% of me, anyway) because I'd taken a workshop in college with Raymond Carver, and I couldn't do what he did. I didn't really know that what he was doing (literary short stories) was clearly different from the kind of thing I wanted to do (e.g., Raymond Chandler). I just thought I didn't have what it takes to be a writer.

Anyway, you wake up one day knowing you have to figure out how to write or something inside you will wither up and die. So I set about to see if writing fiction could be learned, and I discovered it could. Along with good writing books and studying bestsellers, I started to get it. And after I got published, I started to teach it.

For me there are few things as enjoyable as learning a new technique, or getting a different perspective on an old one.

It's kind of like golf. Golfers are always tinkering with their game, trying things out, seeing what works. It can begin, if you don't watch it, to drive you a little bit mad. As you're getting ready to tee off, you might find yourself thinking of the 22 most important things at point of impact-- and immediately freeze up.

Which brings me to the point of this post. When you write, you have to write freely. You can't let a lot of craft knowledge freeze you up.

Sometimes, those who are writing their next novel put too much stress on all the things they think they should be doing, and end up not doing much of anything.

When you write, write. And try to get a first draft done as quickly as possible. It's best to concentrate on only a few basics and just *go*.

1. Make sure the stakes are high enough for the Lead. I advocate "death overhanging" as being the key to this. There are three kinds of death: physical, professional and psychological. If you look at the most popular novels out there, one or all of these are at work in the plot.

2. Make sure the opposition to the Lead is stronger than the Lead. Only then will readers truly be "worried" enough to read on.

3. Make sure your individual scenes are packed with tension or conflict. That means you never have a scene where everything is hunky-dory. At all times, in some way or other, there is worry, fear or outright confrontation.

And that's about it. There will be more work to be done, of course. Especially upon revision. But as you go through your first draft, let these fundamentals guide you. Don't freeze up thinking about myriad things.

Just go.

It's between writing stints that you study and learn and adjust. A good golf teacher will tell you never to work on your swing in the middle of a round. Finish the round, and *then* go over to the practice tee and work on things. Review your fundamentals, and if need be consult a teaching professional.

Keep learning, keep practicing, but when you write, write like it's play. Get caught up in what you're doing.

Backstory

You will find those who argue that there should be no backstory at all in your first chapters. Why not? Because, by definition, backstory is what has happened before your narrative opens, and you want to establish the action first, get the readers locked in on that.

This is, on the surface, sound advice. These days we do not have the leisure time, a la Dickens, to set the stage and do a ton of narrative summary up front. Or, a la Michener, begin with the protozoa of the pre-Cambrian earth and record their evolutionary development into the Texans of today.

I am a firm believer in beginning with action (which doesn't mean, necessarily, car chases or gun fights). The best openings, IMO, show a character *in motion*. And further, manifesting a "disturbance" to their ordinary world.

I tell writing students, "Act first, explain later." A big mistake in many manuscripts is that chapter one carries too much exposition. The writer thinks the reader has to know a bunch of character background to understand the action. Mistake. Readers will wait a long time for the explanations when there's a character in motion, facing a disturbance.

However, I am a strong advocate of strategic backstory in

the opening. I say *strategic* because you do have a strategy in your opening, one above all — bond your character with the reader.

Without that character bonding, readers are not going to care about the action, at least not as much as they should. Backstory, properly used, helps you get them into the character so there is an emotional connection. Fiction, above all, should create an emotional experience.

I also stress *properly used*. That means marbled within the action, not standing alone demanding to be read.

The guys who do this really well also happen to be two of the bestselling novelists of our time, King and Koontz. You think that's just a coincidence?

So here's the simple "rule." Start with action. Let's see a character in motion, doing something. Make sure there's some trouble, even minor, on the page (disturbance) and then you can give us bite-sized bits, or several paragraphs (if you write them well!) of backstory.

An early Koontz (when he was using the pseudonym Leigh Nichols) is *Twilight*. It opens with a mother and her six-year-old son at a shopping mall (after an opening line that portends trouble, of course). On page one Koontz drops this in:

To Christine, Joey sometimes seemed to be a little old man in a six-year-old boy's small body. Occasionally he said the most amazingly grown-up things, and he usually had the patience of an adult, and he was often wiser than his years.

But at other times, especially when he asked where his daddy was or why his daddy had gone away--or even

when he *didn't* ask but just stood there with the question shimmering in his eyes—he looked so innocent, fragile, so heartbreakingly vulnerable that she just had to grab him and hug him.

Koontz bonds us with this Lead through sympathy. We don't know why the boy's father isn't there, but we don't have to know right away, do we? In this way Koontz also creates a little mystery which makes us want to keep on reading.

Now, a word of warning when writing in first person POV. It's much easier for the narrator to give us a backstory dump. But the "rule" remains the same, act first, explain later. To see how it's done, check out the opening chapter of Harlan Coben's *Gone for Good*, which begins:

Three days before her death, my mother told me – these weren't her last words, but they were pretty close – that my brother was still alive.

We then cut to the mother's funeral, and the narrator, Will Klein, leaving the house to walk through his old neighborhood. He has a specific place he's going, the place where a terrible murder happened years before. Along the way he describes the setting and drops in some backstory, especially about one night when his big brother explained the "facts of life" to him from a ninth grader's perspective. It's a warm, human bit that creates sympathy. But Coben weaves it in with the action, which is about the narrator getting to the murder spot. That happens on the very next page. Very little time is lost to backstory.

Some time ago I interviewed Laura Caldwell, author of the Izzy McNeil series. She told me the following:

"I wish I'd known how to weave in background information instead of dumping it in big chunks. It's still something I struggle with, although I think I've improved a lot. It's a skill that has to constantly be refined so the background information which gets delivered reads and feels organic right at that point in the story."

Good point from Laura.
Here's an example from Try Dying. Ch. 1 is about a bizarre death. Ch. 2 opens with the narrator in action, facing opposition (disturbance). A hugely successful lawyer named Barton Walbert. It's a deposition. About four paragraphs in:

I was a pup compared to Walbert. He was fifty-three and in his prime. At thirty-four, I was just hitting my stride. But the arrogance of youth is a good thing for trial lawyers. Like the young gun who comes to town looking for the aging outlaw, wanting to test the best, I was loaded and ready.

I wanted to slip in the age and the attitude. Then I get back to the action. It's quite enough for this scene.

Consider Your Worth: Backstory

1. Take a look at your opening chapter. Highlight all backstory.

2. Assess how much you've put in. Take out anything that does not contribute to some emotional connection with the character. Move that material to a later chapter.

3. If you have no backstory, write some up in a separate document, free form. Then take some of that and put it in, a little at a time, in the opening chapter. Look for anything that gives us empathy or sympathy with the character.

Pro and Con

For the September, 2010 issue of *Writers Digest,* I was asked to participate on a feature with nine other writing experts. We'd each take a position on a well known writing "rule." The another expert would be matched up taking the opposite side.

It was a great idea, a lot of fun. It helped me think things through again. I was given the choice of one pro and one con. Below are the subjects I selected.

PRO: Turn Off Your Inner Editor
Writing is a lot like golf, only without the beautiful scenery and checkered pants.

To get any good at the game you have to practice like mad, usually under the watchful eye of a good teacher. You have to think a thousand little thoughts as you work on your various shots.

But when you get out on the course you must put all those thoughts aside. If you don't, you'll freeze up. You'll play rigid.

What you have to do is train yourself to go with the flow and the feel, trusting what you've learned. *After* a round is the time to think about what went wrong and devise ways to practice on the weak areas.

Same goes for writing. You have to write freely when you write, and think about the craft afterward. Write your scene without overthinking it. Let the characters live and breathe.

After you're done, read it over and fix things. I like to check my previous day's work, edit it lightly, then move on.

Study writing books and articles, get feedback from readers or a critique group. But when you write, write. That's how you truly learn the craft.

Practice writing for five or ten minutes without stopping. Write anything—essays, journal entries, prose poems, diatribes, stream-of-consciousness memoirs, letters to yourself.

You'll soon learn to keep that inner editor at bay when you're actually writing your fiction.

And the best part is you don't have to wear checkered pants to do it.

CON: Write Every Day

Don't write every day.

I'm a big believer in word quotas. One of the earliest, and perhaps still the best pieces of advice I ever got was to set a quota of words and stick to it. I used to do a daily count.

But a thing called life would intrude and I'd miss a day. Or there were times when writing seemed like playing tennis in the La Brea tar pits and that'd be another day I'd miss.

Such days would leave me surly and hard to live with.

Then I switched to a weekly quota and have used it ever since. That way, if I miss a day, I don't beat myself up. I write a little extra on the other days. I use a spreadsheet to keep track and add up my word count for the week.

I also intentionally take one day off a week. I call it my

writing Sabbath. I find that taking a one day break charges my batteries like nothing else. Sunday is the day I've chosen. On Monday I'm refreshed and ready to go. Plus, my projects have been cooking in my subconscious. The boys in the basement, as Stephen King puts it, are hard at work while I'm taking time off.

I also advocate taking a whole week break from writing each year. Use this time to assess your career, set goals, make plans — because if you aim at nothing, there's a very good chance you'll hit it.

How to Benefit from NaNoWriMo

So what is NaNoWriMo? It's an annual event taking place in the month of November. The goal is to produce a 50,000 work novel in one month. It's not going to be perfect or even publishable. There will be a lot of revising to do. But it's a great way to do what writers are supposed to do anyway--write. I tried it, and loved the experience.

The discipline confirmed some lessons in the craft, and gave me new insights on others. So here's my top 10 tips from NaNo, which I think will help you, whatever your normal pace.

1. Loosen Up

If we're not careful with our writing we can get too tentative about it. We write too carefully at times. The old "inner editor" gets bolder and louder. Writing fast under a looming deadline forces you to free yourself. Which is a good thing. Even now, after NaNo, I feel my normal daily writing is a little freer. For this reason alone, NaNo was worth it.

2. Study the Craft

I benefitted from having novel structure wired into me. For example, whenever I'd reach a point where I wasn't sure what to write, I'd take a moment and think about my Lead character's objective. Then I'd start a scene where the Lead takes steps to solve the problem. I'd find the material coming to me as I needed it.

Lesson: Keep studying the craft when you're not writing. Then when you start putting down the words, you'll be doing some of the right things by instinct. We don't tell somebody to just go out to the golf course and start swinging. You can kill somebody that way. We try to get them to practice and drill, and then try to have some fun when actually playing.

3. Bring in the Unexpected

When writing a scene, if things were slowing down or conflict was lagging, I'd ask the boys in the basement to send up something that was the equivalent of Raymond Chandler's admonition to just "bring in a guy with a gun."

Peter Dunne, author of *Emotional Structure,* gives similar advice. "If you think things are slowing down then throw something at your hero that forces him to run like hell."

I did this a number of times and it worked every time.

4. Don't Be Afraid to Skip Around in Your First Draft

I would sometimes leave one scene and jump to another scene and work on that. Then I'd go back to the previous scene and find my mind had been working on it subconsciously.

I had a special folder in Scrivener called "Random Scenes." This is where I'd start writing a scene that came to mind, but had no idea where it would go. Some of my best writing is there, and will find its way into the book.

5. Write Everywhere

I wrote mostly in my home office, but sometimes I'd strap my AlphaSmart to my back and walk or ride my bike to Starbucks and work there for awhile. I had a doctor's appointment, and tapped out 300 words in the waiting room. I wrote on the subway going downtown, and in my car waiting in a parking lot. Even on a treadmill desk I rigged up.

I snatched time, rested, snatched more time. Taking breaks was important between intense spurts. I'd lie on the floor with my feet up for ten or fifteen minutes. Then I'd put on rock music or suspense soundtracks and pump up the volume and write.

Those of you who have trouble finding time to write, cut out some non-essentials. Do you really have to watch *Dancing With the Stars?* And then snatch time to write.

6. Like Voting in Chicago, Write Early and Often

Get as much writing done as you can, as early as you can. I tell writers to follow the "Nifty 350" or "Furious 500" plan. That is, get 350 or 500 words done the very first thing in morning. Get them out of the way, and your quota seems less daunting.

7. Don't Be Afraid

By its very design, NaNoWriMo forces you to let the story lead. You're not always going to be able to stick to a plan. Even if you're an outliner by nature, you have to be ready for organic rabbit trails to emerge in front of you, and have the courage to follow them. But if you do, you're liable to find gold at the end.

8. Journal Daily

Keep a running journal. Sue Grafton does this for all her books. It's like a letter you type to yourself each day, asking where you are in the story, jotting down some ideas that have percolated in the night. Just five minutes of this is worth it. You stimulate something in your mind this way, and get ideas you don't get by just waiting around.

9. Let Things Cool Before You Revise

That's what I'm doing right now. I'll print out a full outline (again, something Scrivener lets you do) then do a read through of my full draft.

10. Enjoy Being a Writer

I said last week that I felt the joy of just pure writing again. That's one of the things I like best about NaNoWriMo. It celebrates the experience and discipline of writing. And we need all the joy we can get to stay with this crazy racket.

My advice to you writers out there is this: start planning

ahead for next November. Give NaNoWriMo a shot. Go to their website, www.nanowrimo.org, and sniff around. Read some of the "pep talks" given by well known authors.

Try it once. Even on the sly. No one will have to know but you.

But I'm betting you'll have fun and will come out of it a better writer.

Interviews

Jeffery Deaver

In the ongoing debate between outliners and seat-of-the pants writers, *New York Times* bestselling author Jeffery Deaver comes down strongly on the outline side.

"The debate is termed in phrases of outlining," Deaver says, "but in fact the real issue is structure. You cannot write an intricate plot-driven novel with multiple, intersecting plots without having an iron-clad structure for the book before you start writing, otherwise you'll be wasting a lot of time and computer space figuring things out as you go."

Even though there are thriller writers who do indeed make it up as they go along, they have to impose a structure somewhere along the line.

"Some people are able to create a structure in their minds and keep it there, but I can't, and I suspect most writers can't. You have to do the work at some point—coming up with pacing and twists and the climactic ending where it all comes together. It's much more efficient to do that first, without the prose getting in the way. Please understand that I'm speaking of purely plot-driven thrillers, like mine. More character oriented, or situation oriented, writers can let the floodgates open and go where the story takes them."

Deaver's legal background also shaped his approach to fiction. "Law school was very helpful in learning to structure a project. No one goes to court or closes a business deal without knowing exactly what will happen ahead of time. A book should be the same. I think the one thing in my background that helped me is more genetic: I have a great curiosity and a very vivid imagination."

That imagination has delivered not just one, but two popular series characters. In Deaver's latest title, *Roadside Crosses,* Kathryn Dance (the series character he's doing on alternate years, with Lincoln Rhyme) makes her second appearance. The keys to a successful series, says Deaver, are "an appealing (though not sentimental) protagonist, somebody who has flaws yet is ultimately morally courageous, a coterie of appealing sidekicks, and some specialty that gives the readers some interesting insights into an aspect of life that they might not be familiar with: Forensics in the case of Lincoln and kinesics (body language) in the case of Kathryn."

The incredibly prolific Deaver is also a master of the short-story-with-a-twist, which is why he has two collections titled *Twisted* and *More Twisted.*

"Short stories are fun to write. But in general they require different sets of skills. Short stories exist (my short stories, that is) exclusively for the twist or surprise; there's no other emotional payoff than that. Novels require the author to load the book with many layers of emotion and come up with plots that will drive the story continuously forward. Like sprinting and marathons: you run in each but the strategy and physiology are very different."

A typical writing day for Deaver is "pretty boring. I work about 8-10 hours day, usually on two books at once. Outlining one, writing the other. Then, as you get a certain level of success, there's a lot of business stuff to do. Interviews, planning tours, making decision on the cover for the Bulgarian large-type edition of the book. You have to do all of that, but the real fun is getting your butt in a chair and writing."

Tess Gerritsen

International bestselling author Tess Gerritsen knows suspense. Her popular thrillers include *Life Support* (1997), *The Surgeon* (2001), *Body Double* (2004), *Vanish* (2005), and *The Mephisto Club* (2006), and her most recent title, *The Bone Garden* (2007). Her books have been translated into 31 languages, and more than 15 million copies have been sold around the world.

Gerritsen maintains a popular blog where she talks about a range of issues from a writer's perspective. Recently, she wrote that "a lot of writers confuse suspense with action." I asked her to expand on that a bit.

"I've always felt that the threat of violence is far more gripping than violence itself," Gerritsen says. "As an example, I think of the film *Aliens,* starring Sigourney Weaver. The most unbearable tension for me during the film was before the monsters had even been located. The Marines knew the creatures were somewhere in the complex, and they could spot signs of an earlier battle between the aliens and the colonists, but the confrontation was still to come. As every nail-biting moment passed, as they advanced into the building, I was on the edge of my seat, waiting for the creatures to appear. The suspense was exquisite."

Once the battle begins, however, the tension dissipates. "But as long as the threat hangs over the characters, as long as you suspect that something awful is going to happen, you're on the edge of your seat. When violence actually occurs, there's nothing more to fear."

Which is why Gerritsen keeps the violence "at bay for as long as possible, while simultaneously maintaining a continual sense of threat."

Gerritsen's technique is hard won. She begins her writing day with coffee and does all her first drafts with pen and paper. " I've tried composing on computer," she says, "and it never works."

Her writing sessions, she explains, are usually accompanied by a lot of sighing, moaning, and sounds of pain. "It's hard for me, and it never gets easier."

But that hard work shows up on the page. One example is her 1995 bestseller, *Vanish*. "There's a scene," Gerritsen says, "where two young women are hidden on the roof and can hear the sounds of murder going on inside the house. Only when things go silent do they dare creep back into the house, and find their housemates slaughtered. They know they need money and warm clothing to make their escape, so they frantically gather those necessities before fleeing. During which you the reader are thinking *get out, get out NOW!* Nothing violent happens to them in that chapter. But because you know the killers could come back any minute -- indeed, the killers could already be watching for them to step out of the house -- you expect the worst."

Gerritsen explains further, "It's the sort of scene, if it were a movie, where you'd hear the nervous tremolo of a violin in the soundtrack. I guess that's how I'd best describe it -- the scene with *something's about to happen* theme music!"

It's that kind of music that keeps readers turning the pages in a Gerritsen novel.

David Morrell

What does it take to make a bestseller these days? In addition to a ripping good read, there's a market reality to consider.

"Publishing changed so much in the past decade," says bestselling author David Morrell (*Long Lost, Creepers, Scavenger*). "The only certainty about bestsellers seems to be that if you're a brand name, you'll probably continue to have bestsellers because your publisher sees an economic benefit in paying chain stores to feature your books in prominent displays."

These displays are rented space, so "aggressive support from the publisher is essential. Without it, you won't get on the list."

Independent bookstores also factor into the bestseller lists, and those stores don't get paid for displays. But it still takes a major push from publishers to make an impact here, Morrell says.

"One hundred or two hundred ARCs aren't going to do it. You need thousands, and that goes back to how much money your publisher is willing to spend to attract attention to you. This is not good news. But knowledge is power. Authors need to learn how to promote themselves and do what their publishers should be doing."

So what *can* a new author do in this climate?

"Learn to promote," Morrell counsels. "The Internet is one way to do this, using viral-marketing techniques. But I think there's no substitute for making friends in the book-store world. It's only natural that a store would pay attention to an author whom the clerks have met and who has made an effort. A while ago, Barry Eisler drove 11,000 miles to visit every book store he could find. It made a huge difference in his sales. For *Creepers*, I drove 5,000 miles and visited something like 73 stores in 10 states."

Morrell's superb book on writing, which was originally titled *Lessons From a Lifetime of Writing*, is going to be re-released by Source Books under a new title: *The Successful Novelist — A Lifetime of Lessons About Writing and Publishing*. It will have a new 5,000 word chapter called "The Novelist as Marketer."

"But never assume that self-promotion will help a terrible book," Morrell reminds us. "Ultimately our task is to write as well as we can."

And one of the perennial problems for the writer is that long middle portion, which can sag. Morrell has some advice.

"I recently had the pleasure of spending several hours with Stephen Cannell, the great television writer who is now a bestselling novelist. He told me that second acts used to give him trouble until he realized that he was spending too much time with his main character and it was time for the villain to make some challenging moves. I thought that was interesting. In a single character, strictly limited viewpoint, the second act can get dull inasmuch as we continue to stay with the same person. But in a viewpoint that changes from character to character, we have the opportunity to freshen the story by giving the villain more attention."

But what if you're writing in first person, or limited third person POV?

"Then the premise needs to be strong enough that the twist in the second act holds our attention," says Morrell. "I think Neil Simon once said that second act problems start in the first act. That's the place to look hard at if the second act drags."

Alex Kava

For Alex Kava, bestselling thriller writer (*A Necessary Evil; Whitewash*), literary inspiration didn't come from the usual murder and mayhem sources. Her favorite novel is Harper Lee's *To Kill a Mockingbird*, followed closely by Willa Cather's *My Antonia*.

"I write from the basic premise that good fiction, no matter what genre, must include compelling characters," Kava says. "No matter how brilliant the plot or how incredible the twist may be, if readers aren't interested in your characters they're not going to stay with you for 300-400 pages."

It's quite a lofty goal, Kava freely admits, to try to create another Atticus Finch or Antonia Shimerda. "But when readers finish my novel, *Whitewash* I hope they remember Miss Sadie, the eighty-one-year-old black woman who helps the protagonist make her escape in a 1947

Shenandoah-green Studebaker. Or Leon, the hitman who keeps screwing up because he swears a Coney Island fortune teller put a curse on him. It's a bonus when readers see the similarities between my character, Charlie Starks in *One False* Move and real-life killer, Charles Starkweather. Six years after my first novel I gave in and wrote an unplanned sequel when readers kept insisting Father Michael Keller to be brought to justice."

Kava writes both stand alone novels and the series character Maggie O'Dell. Although she hadn't planned on writing a series –– "for a while I felt like I was learning on the job" –– she does feel she made the right decision in using the third person point of view. "I'm able to bring in other POVs, not just Maggie's. It keeps each novel fresh for me, so I don't feel like I'm stuck with only Maggie. In *Exposed* (due out in October) R.J. Tully, Maggie's partner, plays a major role. Maggie is always the focus but the readers get to see different perspectives of her through other characters."

The biggest challenge in a series book is that "the story doesn't end on the last page. You need to wrap things up with each book so the readers are satisfied, but at the same time, you have to leave them anxious for more."

Kava is the sort of writer who has a consistent theme running through her work. "I'm constantly examining that fine line between good and evil," she sais. "I want to see what people are capable of. What are we willing to do to survive, to not get caught, to preserve our reputations, to save our lives, to save a loved one's life? It's been said that everyone shows his or her true character when pushed to the edge. That's what I like to do. Push and shove my characters to the edge and then see what they're capable of doing."

I asked Kava about her typical writing day. "There lies the problem," she told me. "There is no typical. In Florida I write on the deck or in my office or by the kitchen counter. In Omaha it's on the screened-in porch or in the writing shed or late at night sitting up in bed. Sometimes I use a stand-up desk because I tend to pace. I write bits and pieces of chapters and dialogue in a notebook. Another notebook has all my research notes. These days I force myself to use a laptop as much as possible because it's quicker, though I swear I think better in longhand. I still do what I like to call my writing marathons. I try to clear my schedule of appointments, distractions, engagements for at least a week at a time and I write from morning until evening. I'm not a coffee drinker but I've been known to guzzle pots of the stuff during my marathons. That's about as typical as I get."

But it all works, as Kava's growing readership attests. Her devotion to the craft creates a reading experience that brings people back for more.

"When the story is over, the last page is read, and the book passed along––if the readers still remember your characters, that's something special."

Brad Thor

International bestselling author Brad Thor writes blazing hot thrillers in the Robert Ludlum tradition. So you might not guess that his literary pedigree includes one T. C. Boyle and the creative writing program at the University of Southern California.

"Tom is a terrific teacher who taught me the mechanics and intricacies of storytelling," Thor explains. "He is not only very talented and extremely bright he's also one hell of a great guy. He's exactly the kind of person you want teaching you creative writing. As students, we created voluminous amounts of fiction in his classes that we work-shopped every week. It was the ideal environment in which to perfect the craft of writing."

How, then, did Thor find himself pursuing the thriller genre?

"It happened after I graduated from USC," he says. "I had moved to Paris, where I studied abroad my junior year, and decided to begin work on a thriller. I got about five chapters into it before packing my laptop up and sending it home. Years later, I realized I had done that because I was afraid of failing. What if I take all this time to write a novel and it doesn't get published or no one likes it?"

Reflecting on that decision now, Thor calls that fear "ridiculous. I've learned that which we are most afraid of pursuing is usually that which we were destined to pursue."

Thor went on to other things, but on his honeymoon his wife asked him what he would regret on his deathbed if he didn't try it.

"I didn't even have to think about it," says Thor. "It was writing a novel and getting it published."

So on their return home, his wife insisted Thor spend two hours of uninterrupted time each day to make his dream come true. "Once that cat was out of the bag, my pride prevented me from running away anymore from what I wanted to do with my life."

Now in the midst of a highly successful career, Thor points to some crucial disciplines he has employed to get there.

"To be a productive writer you have to have an iron will. I have a goal of 2500 words per day which is about five single-spaced pages. As soon as the quota is hit, I get to go do something else, but during a typical day I am normally at my desk the entire time."

Another professor Thor had at USC, Stanley Ralph-Ross, taught him never to end the day at the end of a chapter. "If that's where I am, I begin the next chapter and try to get a couple of sentences into it. This way I'm not worried about where I should go next, I am already there. When I arrive at my desk the next day, the wheels are already spinning and I'm excited about where my thriller is going."

And Thor is passionate about *feeling* his books as he writes. "If I'm not completely on edge and excited by what I'm writing, why should I expect my readers to be? When someone reads one of my thrillers, they are giving me one of the most precious commodities they have – their time. That's something they can never get back, so I see it as my #1 obligation to give them the most intense ride I am capable of. I want their palms sweating, their heart beating, the telephone ringer turned off, and all responsibilities all but ignored because they can't put down my book."

That excitement has resulted in Thor's popular series character, Scot Harvath, and in a freshness from book to book.

"I like to reveal a bit more about Harvath in every novel. He is a Navy SEAL who gets recruited to the Secret Service to help bolster the White House's counter and anti-terrorism capabilities and soon becomes the President's favorite go-to-guy for difficult, off-the-books operations.

"I like to put Harvath in situations I know will be challenging and uncomfortable for him. I like him to be forced to use his brain as much as his brawn to get out of situations and overcome obstacles. I strive to keep him interesting and to use who he is and what he does to reveal fascinating pieces of information to my readers.

"At the end of the day, my readers are some of the brightest people out there and I continually strive to raise the bar of my writing to keep them engrossed and entertained and to keep challenging myself. I always begin a new novel by saying, 'This is going to be very exciting. How do we go further than with the last book?'"

When it comes to advice for new writers, Thor does not hesitate. "To be a great writer you *have* to be a great reader. Know what is out there in your genre. Why are other people so well-reviewed? What do their readers love about their plots, settings, and characters? What books on the art of writing can help you take yours to the next level?"

He also knows what "rule" not to follow. "The worst piece of writing advice you will ever hear is 'write what you know.' If that were actually true, we wouldn't have a J.K. Rowling, a Ray Bradbury. I tell people – *write what you love to read.* That's where your passion is and that's where you'll find your success as an author."

Michael Palmer

When Michael Palmer, M.D., first thought about writing a medical thriller, his sister offered a dissenting view. "You're dull," she said.

"One of my younger (I have two of them) sisters' missions

has always been to keep me right-sized," Palmer explains. "That hasn't always been easy. When my first book (*The Sisterhood*) made the *New York Times* list, one of them had 500 business cards made up for me with my name on them and underneath: MINOR LITERARY FIGURE."

Well, this "figure" has only gone on to write a dozen *Times* bestsellers. But he had a lot to learn to get there.

"I have always been many things," says Palmer. "Scattered, distracted, imaginative, goofy, intense, withdrawn, expansive, caring, disciplined, forgetful, adventurous, technophobic, funny, frustrating, and predictably unpredictable.....but never dull. What I have done since that first year is, I have grown as a writer. Except for some English and literature courses at Wesleyan, I never had any formal training in writing--especially creative writing. My agent Jane Rotrosen actually took less money for my first book so that I could work with the legendary editor (now, the late) Linda Gray at Bantam. She line-edited my first four or five drafts of *The Sisterhood*, and taught me editorial adjectives such as 'mawkish' and its nasty little cousin, 'purple.' She taught me how to use rewrites to choose better words and how to carefully avoid (split infinitive intentional) those passages that I think say to the reader, 'Hey, look what a great writer I am. . . . How inventive and clever.' Samuel Johnson is quoted as saying that the secret to good literary style is to take those words and sentences and paragraphs you are particularly fond of, and get rid of them immediately. Linda and my subsequent editor Beverly Lewis never stopped teaching me that."

Writing high concept thrillers is a challenge, Palmer notes, because great ideas are not easy to come by. So he has consciously developed other aspects of his writing craft.

"I feel like I may never come up with an idea for a book as strong as that for *The Sisterhood*, so the trick for me has been to write a better richer book about an idea that may not be as strong. I am always looking for medical ethical issues to write fiction about. My newer books have more and stronger subplots, and a number of them have multiple story threads and protagonists. Examples are *Fatal* and *The Fifth Vial*, each of which has three main characters and three intertwining plot lines. I also feel as if my writing is getting more clean-edged and less intrusive. Also, I am not afraid to accept evil for the sake of evil, and not merely as a manifestation of overzealous commitment to a cause or ideal. One other change is that I no longer feel I have to explain everything to the reader. Even though it annoys some people to not know whether Jessie and Alex end up together in *The Patient*, or Natalie and Ben in *The Fifth Vial*, I'm more happy than I once was to 'encourage' readers to figure those things out for themselves."

On his website, www.michaelpalmerbooks.com, Palmer generously shares writing tips for budding novelists. One of these is the Hitchcockian notion of "The McGuffin."

"The concept of the McGuffin is a fun one to learn about and master. In truth I believe that the next thing a thriller writer needs after a strong 'What if?' and before a 'Whose book is it and why?' is a McGuffin. It is essentially the answer to the 'What if?' and can be changed if a better McGuffin crops up. However, if your What if? is 'What if the president of the United States disappears while giving a speech in front of 100,000 people and a worldwide TV audience of millions?' then you as a writer had better have a damn good explanation as to how that happened. That's your McGuffin. No decent McGuffin, no book. Aliens beamed him up? Well, okay, if that's the best you can do, let's go with it."

I asked Palmer about his typical writing day.

"I start at 5:15 a.m. by flossing (always floss, everyone), then meditating (20 minutes), then spending 45 minutes getting my kid (17) up, breakfasted and off to the bus for school. Then I clean the kitchen, make coffee, read the paper (15 minutes, mostly the sports), and finally take my second cup of joe up to my study where, by 8:30 I have answered a few e-mails and started writing. The more I know what I am doing, the more time I can spend doing it. Five to six pages a day is my goal. After five hours I often begin to get loopy. Then I begin taking breaks and answering more e-mails. By mid afternoon I am asleep in my desk chair, hoping the phone will ring and wake me up."

David Baldacci

Most people might describe David Baldacci is a "lawyer turned novelist" (and one of the most successful, too). But that is not entirely accurate. It's more like Baldacci is a reader who wanted to write, and kept up that dream during law school and after.

"I was a library rat as a kid and I loved books that captured me for days in the wonderful world of words," Baldacci explains. "I wanted to do that for others. Then all through law school and after becoming a practicing attorney, I was writing. So the leap from lawyer to full time writer didn¹t need much motivation."

Nor did he need much of a leap to get to the top of the bestseller lists. It didn't hurt that his first novel, *Absolute Power*, was turned into a hit Clint Eastwood movie. But it also helped that Baldacci is a craftsman who takes his writing seriously.

"Building characters with depth and dialogue that 'rings true' are the keys to what I consider a great novel. Also I've gotten smarter about research and knowing what to leave in and what to cut. I don't write textbooks and a writer has to fight the impulse to leave all his hard research work in the book. It invariably kills the narrative drive of the story."

No problem with narrative drive in Baldacci's body of work. His latest hardcover, *First Family*, debuted at #1 on the New York Times Bestseller list, and the paperback of *The Whole Truth* has spent thirteen weeks on the Times extended Mass Market list.

I asked Baldacci if he is an "outliner" or "seat of the pantser" when it comes to plotting.

"Really, a bit of both. I do mini-outlines at the beginning of a project. Once I get about 150 pages into the novel, I have a good feel to where the characters are taking me. I may have a plot twist or two sketched out but at this point in the book, I am letting the story take me for the ride."

So what would you guess Baldacci's typical writing day is like? Highly structured, as one might expect from a former DC power lawyer?

"No, it's completely atypical. And honestly, I think as a writer, it has to be that way, at least for me. Routine can be the kiss of death for the creative process. And then it becomes too much like a job instead of a passion."

Carla Neggers

Writers, of course, come from an infinite variety of

backgrounds. I know a successful author who did not read books growing up. Others read voraciously, or started writing stories as soon as they could form letters with crayons.

But I have never met a writer who started writing in a tree. Until New York Times bestselling author Carla Neggers.

"I grew up in the country with six brothers and sisters," Neggers says, "and we all loved to climb trees. I'd grab a pad and pen and scoot up to my favorite branch in a sugar maple and sit up there and write. It was a great place to be on my own with my muse! I suspect it says that I have a zest for adventure and don't like to be tied to a computer. And that I can write anywhere, anytime. I also used to write on a rock in the middle of a brook."

Neggers, like many romantic suspense writers today, cut her teeth on category romances. This was, for her, an invaluable learning experience.

"Not only did I learn a lot, I met some wonderful people and worked with some fantastic editors. In terms of the craft of writing, I learned more about how 'internal' conflict -- within and between characters -- can drive and enrich a story. I also unleashed my sense of humor. Most of my category romances are funny books!"

Obviously, Neggers has learned her craft well. Publishers Weekly calls her just released title, *Betrayals,* "highly entertaining" and "a believable, gripping story that will keep armchair sleuths guessing."

So what is her technique for keeping readers in suspense? Whatever keeps things moving.

"When someone asks me if I'm an outliner or a seat-of-the-pants writer, I say yes. I don't have a set technique. It depends on the book. A synopsis is a jumping off point for me. I do best when I focus on what I call the forward momentum of the story versus forcing myself to write a certain way. If forward momentum means stopping and outlining, I stop and outline. If it means going back to Page 1 and rewriting, I go back to Page 1 and rewrite. If it means writing in a whoosh without pausing to revise...that's what I do. I'm disciplined as a writer but not regimented. For me, plotting is integrated with everything else about the story, but I often will do a chapter-by-chapter outline of the book in columns on a single page. That way I can see the story as a whole. It's very visual. I can see pacing, major plot points, the development of various plot threads...it helps me see the forest and not just the trees!"

One thing Neggers is known for is her character work. How does she make her story people memorable?

"I see them as real people in my head. *The Widow, The Angel* and my upcoming novel, *The Mist*, are connected books, and for me, the heroines -- Abigail Browning, Keira Sullivan and Lizzie Rush -- are all individuals. I can no more confuse them with each other than I could my own brothers and sisters. The same with Owen Garrison, Simon Cahill and Will Davenport. I don't think of myself as constructing characters so much as I do as allowing characters to reveal themselves to me."

Liker her plots, Neggers' writing day is uniquely structured. It's a matter of forward momentum according to the needs of the developing story.

"I believe in the yin-yang of periods of concentration and periods of abandonment (or *simmer time*). At the start of a book, I often work shorter hours because I need to walk away and let things simmer. At the end of a book, I get in the 'zone' and write much longer hours -- more concentration, less abandonment. That said, I'm a morning person. I try to avoid non-writing time sinks in the morning. Note that key word 'try'!"

Eric Van Lustbader

There are some novelists who write with a common theme, a "what" that drives their fiction. Others discover the "what" as they go along.

International bestselling author Eric Van Lustbader doesn't so much write with a "what" in mind, but a "who."

He calls this The Outsider.

"Since I'm an Outsider myself," Lustbader explains, "all my protagonists are Outsiders, as well, starting with Nicholas Linnear [of the Ninja Cycle novels]. Being half-Asian, half-Western, he belongs in neither world. He stands apart and, like all Outsiders, is more qualified to comment on society. Because he has no biases, no axes to grind, his observations are neutral, therefore balanced, most truthful and thought-provoking."

In addition to his numerous creations, Lustbader has also carried on the saga of Jason Bourne, in cooperation with the Robert Ludlum estate. The same Outsider motif drew Lustbader to Bourne.

"Many's the time Bob Ludlum and I would discuss our respective prototypical heroes," says Lustbader, "remarking on how similar in makeup they were: loners yet fiercely loyal, they were walking, talking oxymorons, which made them special not only to the two of us, but to our millions of readers. Because aren't human beings, by nature, paradoxical? Think about it. How many times have you found yourself experiencing two opposite emotions simultaneously? We wonder how we can love and hate someone at the same time, but that's rational thinking; emotions like love and hate are irrational, not subject to the artificial 'laws' humans have imposed on society, in a futile attempt to turn chaos into order."

In the forthcoming *First Daughter* (Forge), Lustbader's protagonist, Jake McClure, survives a horrific upbringing. His inner scars drive him to the outside, and raises a central question that Lustbader sees as having wide significance.

"When you're so deeply damaged, how do you let in even those you love? This is a question that haunts Jack, but I think, to some extent, it haunts a lot of people."

Lustbader is one of the few novelists who is a major success in two
different genres (fantasy and thrillers). But the craft he brings to each is uniform.

"Fiction writing is fiction writing, no matter the genre. What I mean is this: all fiction is grounded in the same basic needs: story arc and character arcs. A story begins with an inciting event: something shocking, something that upends the protagonist's world. Think of *North By Northwest*. Cary Grant plays a mild-mannered advertising executive waiting for his mother in a hotel lobby. Just as the bellboy comes around calling the name of what turns out to be the fictitious name of a spy the CIA has concocted, he waves to someone he thinks is his mother. Now a rival group of spies is convinced he's the fictional character. Everything in the film proceeds from that premise. That's the story arc."

And the character arc?

"Again, let's look at the Cary Grant character in *North By Northwest*. When we first meet him he's a momma's-boy drone (despite the fact that he looks like Cary Grant!). Because of the inciting event, he will move from being a disbelieving nerd to a man on the run, a man who begins to use his mind to escape the enemy's ever more clever traps, until at the end, he becomes a reluctant spy for the CIA and a hero by defeating the enemy spy ring. Oh, yes, and along the way he falls in love. The changes he undergoes from the beginning to the end of the film comprise his character arc. One of the main points of a character arc is that the hero goes from being passive (events happen to him) to being the initiator, a central attribute of a hero in any genre.

"These priorities are fiction-driven, rather than genre-driven."

I asked Lustbader what he does differently today than when he started.

"I think it's more a question of attitude than of action. I have more experience, for one thing, so constructing a storyline that I find exciting is a familiar task, though possibly not any easier. For another, I'm more confident, and confidence brings about concentration, which any writer must have. Also, I'm better able to apportion my time.

"That said, I'm still obsessed with writing. When I'm in the middle of a project it doesn't matter whether I write one paragraph or eight pages, my head is filled with my story and my characters 24/7. It's sort of like being possessed, and I have to say sometimes the grip of it is still sometimes frightening, but this is the only way I can write, walking the edge between one world and the other. Much of the time, especially toward the end of a novel, the world I've created is far more real to me than life; it also seems far more interesting."

This "obsessive" approach means there is no "typical" writing day for Lustbader.

"The word 'typical' is not in my vocabulary. Right from the get-go I was taught to think independently, to think outside the box, and, most importantly, to see the big picture. As I've already said, I'm thinking about a project 24/7. That means, for instance, I always have a pad and pen beside my bed. Invariably, in the midst of a novel, I'll have a fistful of thoughts the moment after I turn out the lights at night."

Lustbader used to write only in the morning, but over the years that's changed. "Now I often don't get started writing until three or four in the afternoon. Why this is, I can't say; writing is a basically irrational experience. And it's hard work, but try telling that to anyone who doesn't write."

Steve Martini

I have a lawyer friend who reads (and reviews) just about every legal thriller there is. I once asked him for his top five of all time, and on that list was *Compelling Evidence* by Steve Martini.

Indeed, Martini is one of the recognized masters of the legal thriller. Since his first novel, *The Simeon Chamber*, appeared in 1987, Martini has continued to write critically acclaimed novels, most of which feature criminal defense attorney Paul Madriani.

But it took a few years after Martini's debut for Madriani to make his.

"I had a contract in hand for a second novel," Martini says, "and that tends to provide confidence, since an editor and publisher have shown they believe in you, and that's contagious. I knew I could produce marketable fiction, but my problem was that I was writing on the side and held a day-job (practicing law) to pay the bills. It was the success of *Compelling Evidence* that allowed me to write full time and made it possible for me to become a professional author."

Being free to write full time, however, did mean Martini thought he knew all there was about page-turning fiction.

"The fact is that I am always learning, and continue to learn with each manuscript I write. To date I have written thirteen novels, an unlucky number to retire on, so I will keep going. Of this number, three books have been non-series, stand-alone thrillers and ten have been part of the Paul Madriani series.

"One of the things I learned over the years was that the voice (first person active) that I had used in the Madriani series was becoming far too confining as the series progressed. I learned that I enjoyed the freedom of the omniscient point of view that I used in the non-series stories. So *Revelation*, the most recent Madriani book, incorporates first person active voice in Madriani scenes, and omniscient third person point of view in those scenes in which Madriani is not present. It worked wonderfully and readers will have a chance to see the result in my forthcoming novel *Guardian of Lies.*"

I asked Martini how extensively he pre-planned Paul Madriani's personal evolution over the course of the series.

And how does he keep the character fresh from book to book?

"Paul has gotten older. His daughter has grown up within the stories. I'm not sure that I ever planned this or even thought about it, but the span and arc of his life seemed to mirror my own pretty closely. Perhaps the greatest attempt to freshen his life comes in the most recent work *Guardian of Lies* in which Madriani leaves the courtroom for a substantial portion of the story. There is much more action, and suspense due to the change of voice and point of view. It is one thing to surprise people with a twist in court or some form of legal jeopardy for Paul or his client. It is another to put his life at risk or the lives of other characters wherein the reader actually witnesses the consequence of violence as is the case in *Guardian*."

So what is a typical writing day in the life of Steve Martini?

"I tend to do a great deal of research for all of my books and then write the actual manuscript in a very compressed period of time. My manuscripts, which are fairly long (130,000 to 150,000 words) are produced in final form in a period of between four and five months. For this reason my writing day is very long and often stretches from late morning until late into the night and as the deadline approaches often into the wee hours of the morning. It can be very intense, but I find that plots that are intricate and involved with numerous twists are often best crafted in a more compressed time frame. It's easier to retain mastery over all of the complex story elements."

Sarah Pekkanen

I met Sarah Pekkanen when she alerted me she was mentioning my book, *Plot & Structure*, in a radio essay for

"All Things Considered" on National Public Radio. I listened in, and not only was it a nice endorsement, she also put me alongside Stephen King and my own agent, Donald Maass, both of whom have superb books on the craft. Pretty heady company. Sarah explained how each of these books helped her along as she wrote her novel, *The Opposite of Me*, released under Simon & Schuster's imprint Washington Square Press.

JSB: Sarah, you had an extensive journalism background before you started writing your novel. Do you see a connection between that kind of writing and writing fiction?

SP: Yes and no. I learned to write on deadline, which is an incredibly valuable skill. Knowing that a newspaper was holding an empty space for my story - and that I'd be out of a job if I didn't consistently fill it - meant I couldn't agonize over every word or succumb to crippling self-doubt. I was lucky in that I moved around to different beats and different cities, covering a wide range of stories - interviews with testy politicians, man-on-the-street reactions to the day's breaking news, and long, rich features. But after my kids were born and I left newspapers to try my hand at fiction, I realized I needed to un-learn some of my habits. Instead of trying to condense a story to fit the space constraints of a newspaper, I needed to find places to expand it. I also had to quiet the cynical part of my brain that constantly questioned whether something in my fiction was realistic, and encourage my imagination to fly.

JSB: *The Opposite of Me* is your first novel. And it sold. This is not the usual path for new writers. What do you think made the difference in this case?

SP: Actually, I started writing books when I was nine or ten years old, and I used to confidently send them off to publishers and wait for the day when I could stroll into a bookstore and see one of my creations - like "The Lost Gold" or "Miscellaneous Tales and Poems" -- on the shelves. After I left my reporting job to stay at home with my young sons, I did write a novel that didn't sell. But it got me a literary agent. So, technically *The Opposite of Me* isn't my first book. But here's what made a difference (and Jim I hope you don't edit this part out!). I found a copy of *Plot & Structure* and my writing improved immensely. Something about the simple, straightforward advice illuminated what I'd been doing wrong in my manuscripts. I wrote *The Opposite of Me* in nine months, and it was sold at auction a week after my agent submitted it. And I continue to pore over *Plot & Structure* as I write my second novel.

JSB: How about literary influences?

SP: I read extensively within my genre - commercial women's fiction - and I also adore mystery. I love writers like Harlan Coben and Jennifer Weiner who weave humor through books with serious themes, and I tried to do that in *The Opposite of Me*. One book that really electrified me is *In Cold Blood*. When I realized that Truman Capote created a book that could stand as masterful piece of fiction - and yet every word was true - I began trying to recreate that technique on a much smaller scale in my newspaper stories. I wrote a number of narratives for papers like The Baltimore Sun, including a piece on a police officer's accidental death at the hands of a fellow officer, and a story about a student at Columbine High School who was transformed from the class clown into a hero who saved lives during the shootings.

JSB: Do you have a typical writing schedule?

SP: I wrote *The Opposite of Me* while my two oldest boys were in school and I was pregnant with my third - so I had lovely long stretches of quiet time in which to walk the dog, brew a pot of tea, and sink into my manuscript. Now things are much more hectic, so I've had to learn to write in little snatches of time as well as big spaces. I'm lucky in that I can usually score a babysitter, and my parents live five minutes away and are always willing to help. I try to write in the mornings for a bit after the big boys go to school, and when the baby is napping. But with this book, I've had to fit writing in around my life rather than the other way around - which isn't such a bad thing.

JSB: Where are you on your next book?

SP: I've already turned it in to my agent, and now I'm tweaking the final draft a bit based on her suggestions. I was advised to begin my second book before my debut came out, and I'm so glad I listened to that advice! Promoting a new book takes an enormous amount of time, and I'm in awe of authors who manage to juggle both jobs and do them well. If I hadn't started my second book last year, I'd have a lot of trouble finding the time to sit down for the big think sessions it takes me to lay out the bare bones of a plot.

JSB: Here's one that's pretty common for published writers, but since you've just hit the shelves your take will be particularly fresh: What's the most important advice you have for new writers out there wanting to break in?

SP: Set a goal - whether it be a paragraph a day or five pages - and figure out how to stick to it. Writing is like exercise: You need to do it nearly every day to get results. Well, at least that's what I've heard. I don't exactly have the exercise thing mastered yet.

Boyd Morrison

Boyd Morrison does not know what he wants to be when he grows up. So along the way in his life's trek he got himself a PhD in industrial engineering, worked on the Space Station Freedom project at Johnson Space Center, got some really tough duty managing an Xbox games group at Microsoft, was and still is a professional actor . . . and, oh yeah, made a little stop on TV to became a *Jeopardy* champion.

One other little item: His hot adventure novel, *The Ark*, published by Simon & Schuster.

Boyd's journey to publication covers about 13 years, and I wanted to interview him for because I saw someone who approached this whole business wisely and systematically. In this interview, along with everything else, you'll find Boyd's tips about getting the most from a conference. Pure gold. Be sure to learn more about Boyd at his

JSB: Publication of your novel, *The Ark*, is a success story with a unique background. How did you get the idea?

BM: Engineers usually get a raw deal in thriller fiction, which is something I pay attention to because I'm an engineer myself. When the strapping hero needs some critical piece of technology to save the world, he turns to an engineer for said object or solution and then proceeds to kick butt (think James Bond getting his gadgets from Q or Captain Kirk demanding more power from Scotty). And I got sick of that, so I decided to cut out the middleman and create an action hero named Tyler Locke who IS an engineer. Nerds rule!

While I was looking for an adventure for Tyler to

swashbuckle through, I saw a documentary on the search for Noah's Ark. I'm a skeptic by nature, so my first thought was, "Yeah right. They're going to find a 6,000-year-old ship intact on a snowy mountaintop." But then I got the inkling of an idea: maybe the reason we've never found Noah's Ark was because we had been deceived all these years as to its true location. And maybe the Ark held such a terrible secret that it could very well mean the end of mankind if it were ever found again. Noah was the first engineer (who else but an engineer could build the Ark?), so it was the perfect object for Tyler to search for.

JSB: How did you get an agent to represent *The Ark*?

BM: *The Ark* was the third book I wrote, so I had already gone through two rounds of rejections from agents (both of those books have since been acquired by Simon & Schuster). But I had gotten pretty good at pitching my novels, and I'm a big believer in meeting agents in person. It's so much easier to get your first three chapters read by an agent when you can put "Requested Materials" on the envelope. So I attended the very first Agentfest at the Thrillerfest conference in 2007.

Today Agentfest is done speed-dating style, but the first Agentfest was more leisurely paced, with an agent sitting at each of the tables during the luncheon session. I was late to the luncheon, so I snagged a seat at the very last table. Irene Goodman, who is a highly regarded agent, was attending because she was looking at extending her client list to include thriller authors. She asked every aspiring author at the table to give her their pitch. I had practiced mine so that I could rattle it off. It went like this:

"A relic from Noah's Ark gives a religious fanatic and his followers a weapon that will let them recreate the effects of the biblical flood, and former combat engineer Tyler Locke has seven days to find the Ark and the secret hidden inside before it's used to wipe out civilization again."

I could have stopped at the words "Noah's Ark" because once she heard them she asked to read the first three chapters. I was still working on my own revisions, so it took a couple of months before it was ready to send to her. She told me later that she started to wonder if I'd forgotten about her, but she was one of the first agents I sent it to (I sent it to my five highest agent choices as a simultaneous submission).

She got the chapters on a Monday, read them right away, and then called me when she was done. That day. I practically keeled over in my chair when I got the phone call because no agent had ever called me before. She said she loved the beginning and asked me if I would mind overnighting the rest of the manuscript (note to aspiring authors: it's a good sign when the agent is that eager to get the manuscript). I told her I'd have to think about...oh, who am I kidding? I was already in the car on the way to the post office before she had finished her question.

Irene received the manuscript on a Tuesday, and I figured it would be at least a week before she got back to me. She called on Thursday. With an offer of representation. This time, I did keel over. But I pulled it together and told her I would have to contact the other agents who had it before I could give her an answer. After a few frantic phone calls to the other agents who had the submission, I called Irene back on Friday and said I would love for her to be my agent.

Again, all of this was in 2007. So for those of you who think getting an agent means a smooth path to publication, I'd like to remind you that it's now 2010. The book that Irene snapped up in five days took three years to get published.

JSB: You have been very good not only about attending the top conferences, but getting the most out of them by meeting people, networking and so on. What tips can you give unpublished writers in this regard?

BM: Virtually every person I know in the writing and publishing industry I met at conferences, so I highly recommend that unpublished writers attend them. I could write twenty pages on writers conferences, but I'll boil it down to a few key points.

Know why you're going
Attending a conference is well worth the time and money when you know what you want to get out of it. If you want to meet agents, going to a conference like Bouchercon or Left Coast Crime will be a waste of time because few agents attend them, and then it's usually to serve on a panel, not to search for prospective clients. But if you want to meet writers and readers, Bcon and LCC are perfect. There are plenty of conferences featuring agents looking for new clients. Check out the back of Writer's Digest magazine for conferences near you.

Don't be afraid
Everyone I've met at conferences was incredibly welcoming to me when I was unpublished. No one looks down on unpublished authors. In fact, they're very encouraging. So go up to people and introduce yourself. You'll probably make many friends, as I have. It doesn't matter if they're writers, agents, editors, or readers. Everybody there wants to meet other people. And one important tip: agents and writers hang out at the hotel bar at night; having a drink with them (or even buying a round) is a great way to hear the best industry stories.

Have your pitch ready

If you're pitching a novel, it needs to be a completed manuscript. Nothing disappoints an agent more to hear the idea for a great novel and then find out it won't be done for another year. Have your novel boiled down to a sentence or two that outlines the premise for the plot and the main character that the reader will be rooting for. Then you can elaborate if and when the agent asks follow-up questions. Memorize the pitch so that you can say it without thinking. If you ramble about your story for five minutes, you're going to confuse agents and make them think your manuscript will be just as rambling.

Be nice

This last point should go without saying, but it needs to be emphasized. Be friendly and polite. Smile. You can introduce yourself to agents even if they're not in a pitch session, but don't follow them into a bathroom or slide your manuscript under a stall (believe or not, this happens). Don't put writers on the spot by asking for blurbs in person. If you get to know them, follow-up later with an email asking if they have time to read your manuscript (don't be offended or take it personally if they don't; published writers are super busy as I've recently discovered first hand).

Have fun

Writing is a solitary business, so enjoy yourself in the supportive community of a conference. Every writer gets their batteries recharged by hearing from other writers who've been through exactly what they're going through and made it as a published author. Those conference memories help keep you going when you're sitting by yourself in front of that white screen.

JSB: Tell us a little about your acting self (that makes about three or four "selves" I count for you).

BM: My acting hobby is the exact opposite of my day job as a writer. Writing is rewarding and fun, but it is not interactive or, for that matter, active. Acting--well, it's right there in the word--gets me up on my feet in a collaborative environment with a lot of other talented people. And it's a blast--I mean, they are called "plays" after all. For some reason, I have a need to perform, usually at great peril of making an idiot of myself. I've done stand-up comedy, musicals, improv, stage productions, commercials, and films. I've even done some print ads, and I appeared on the packaging for an herbal tea while wearing a space helmet (you think I'm joking, but I'm not).

Plays are my favorite. There's nothing better than getting that audience reaction when you make them laugh or cry or gasp in surprise. For me, comedies are the most fun. I've done some of the classics, including *Noises Off, The Importance of Being Earnest, and Barefoot in the Park.* Last year, I appeared in Leading Ladies, a Tootsie-style play featuring yours truly trying to pass himself off as a woman to get an inheritance. And I just finished a five-week run in *Rumors* by Neil Simon, a farce in which I played a politician who keeps putting his foot in his mouth.

ABOUT THE AUTHOR

JAMES SCOTT BELL is the author of the #1 bestseller for writers, *Plot & Structure*, and numerous thrillers, including *Deceived, Try Dying* and *Watch Your Back*. His novella *One More Lie* was the first independently published work to be nominated for a prestigious International Thriller Writers Award. Under the pen name K. Bennett, he is also the author of the Mallory Caine zombie legal thriller series, which begins with *Pay Me in Flesh*. He served as the fiction columnist for Writer's Digest magazine and has written highly popular craft books for Writer's Digest Books, including : *Revision & Self-Editing, The Art of War for Writers* and *Conflict & Suspense*.

Jim taught writing at Pepperdine University and at numerous writers conferences in the United States, Canada and Great Britain. He attended the University of California, Santa Barbara where he studied writing with Raymond Carver. He graduated with honors from the University of Southern California law school

He lives in Los Angeles. His website is:

www.JamesScottBell.com.

Made in the USA
Monee, IL
03 March 2025

13393479R00115